Anonymous

The Boy's Book of Ballads

Anonymous

The Boy's Book of Ballads

ISBN/EAN: 9783744774871

Printed in Europe, USA, Canada, Australia, Japan

Cover: Foto ©Thomas Meinert / pixelio.de

More available books at **www.hansebooks.com**

THE BOY'S

BOOK OF BALLADS.

ILLUSTRATED WITH
SIXTEEN ENGRAVINGS ON WOOD FROM DRAWINGS
BY JOHN GILBERT.

*"I never heard the old song of Percie and Douglas, that I found not
my heart moved more than with a trumpet."*—SIR PHILIP SIDNEY.

LONDON:
BELL AND DALDY, 186, FLEET STREET.
MDCCCLXI.

LONDON:
R. CLAY, PRINTER, BREAD STREET HILL.

CONTENTS.

iv *Contents.*

ILLUSTRATIONS.

b

ROBIN HOOD AND GUY OF GISBORNE.

HEN shaws* be sheen,† and swards full fair,
    And leaves both large and long,
It is merry walking in the fair forest
    To hear the small birds' song.

The woodweel‡ sang, and would not cease,
    Sitting upon the spray,
So loud, he wakened Robin Hood,
    In the greenwood where he lay.

Now by my faith, said jolly Robin,
    A sweaven§ I had this night ;
I dreamt me of two wight yeomen,
    That fast with me can fight.

* Woods.   † Shining.   ‡ A kind of thrush.   § Dream.

Methought they did me beat and bind,
　　And took my bow me fro';
If I be Robin alive in this land,
　　I'll be wroken* on them two.

Sweavens are swift, master, quoth John,
　　As the wind that blows o'er a hill;
For if it be never so loud this night,
　　To-morrow it may be still.

Busk ye, bowne† ye, my merry men all,
　　And John shall go with me,
For I'll go seek yon wight‡ yeomen,
　　In the greenwood where they be.

Then they cast on their gowns of green,
　　And took their bows each one,
And they away to the green forest,
　　A shooting forth are gone;

Until they came to the merry greenwood,
　　Where they had gladdest be,
There were they aware of a wight yeoman,
　　His body leaned to a tree.

* Revenged.　　　† Make ready.　　　‡ Strong.

A sword and a dagger he wore by his side,
　Of many a man the bane;
And he was clad in his capull* hide
　Top and tail and mane.

Stand you still, master, quoth Little John,
　Under this tree so green,
And I will go to yon wight yeoman
　To know what he doth mean.

Ah! John, by me thou settest no store,
　And that I fairly find;
How oft send I my men before,
　And tarry myself behind?

It is no cunning a knave to ken,
　An† a man but hear him speak;
An it were not for bursting of my bow,
　John, I thy head would break.

As often words they breeden bale,‡
　So they parted, Robin and John;
And John is gone to Barnesdale:
　The gates§ he knoweth each one.

---

* Horse-hide.　　† If.　　‡ Mischief.　　§ Ways.

But when he came to Barnesdale,
  Great heaviness there he had,
For he found two of his own fellows
  Were slain both in a glade.

And Scarlett he was flying a-foot
  Fast over stock and stone,
For the proud sheriff with seven score men
  Fast after him is gone.

One shot now I will shoot, quoth John,
  (With Christe his might and main ;)
I'll make yon fellow that flies so. fast,
  To stop he shall be fain.

Then John bent up his long bende-bow,
  And fettled* him to shoot :
The bow was made of tender bough,
  And fell down to his foot.

Woe worth, woe worth thee, wicked wood
  That ere thou grew on a tree ;
For now this day thou art my bale,
  My boote† when thou shouldst be.

* Made ready.   † Help.

Guy of Gisborne.

His shoot it was but loosely shot,
    Yet flew not the arrow in vain,
For it met one of the sheriff's men,—
    Good William-a-Trent was slain.

It had been better for William-a-Trent ,
    To have been a-bed with sorrow,
Than to be that day in the greenwood glade
    To meet with Little John's arrow.

But as it is said, when men be met,
    Five can do more than three,
The sheriff hath taken Little John,
    And bound him fast to a tree.

Thou shalt be drawn by dale and down,
    And hang'd high on a hill.
But thou mayst fail of thy purpose, quoth John,
    If it be Christe his will.

Let us leave talking of Little John,
    And think of Robin Hood,
How he is gone to the wight yeoman,
    Where under the leaves he stood.

Good morrow, good fellow, said Robin so fair,
 Good morrow, good fellow, quoth he :
Methinks by this bow thou bear'st in thy hand,
 A good archer thou shouldst be.

I am wilful* of my way, quo' the yeoman,
 And of my morning tide.
I'll lead thee through the wood, said Robin ;
 Good fellow, I'll be thy guide.

I seek an outlaw, the stranger said,
 Men call him Robin Hood ;
Rather I'd meet with that proud outlaw
 Than forty pounds so good.

Now come with me, thou wighty yeoman,
 And Robin thou soon shalt see :
But first let us some pastime find
 Under the greenwood tree.

First let us some mastery make
 Among the woods so even,
We may chance to meet with Robin Hood
 Here at some unset† steven.

   * Missing.   † Unexpectedly.

They cut them down two summer shoggs,*
    That grew both under a briar,
And set them threescore rod, in twain,
    To shoot the pricks† y-fere.‡

Lead on, good fellow, quoth Robin Hood,
    Lead on, I do bid thee.
Nay by my faith, good fellow, he said,
    My leader thou shalt be.

The first time Robin shot at the prick,
    He miss'd but an inch it fro';
The yeoman he was an archer good,
    But he could never shoot so.

The second shoot had the wighty yeoman,
    He shot within the garlànd ;§
But Robin he shot far better than he,
    For he clave the good prick-wand.

A blessing upon thy heart, he said ;
    Good fellow, thy shooting is good ;
For an thy heart be as good as thy hand,
    Thou wert better than Robin Hood.

* Twigs.   † Marks.   ‡ Together.   § A ring round the prick

Now tell me thy name, good fellow, said he,
    Under the leaves of lyne.*
Nay, by my faith, quoth bold Robin,
    Till thou have told me thine.

I dwell by dale and down, quoth he,
    And Robin to take I'm sworn ;
And when I am called by my right name,
    I am Guy of good Gisbòrne.

My dwelling is in this wood, says Robin,
    By thee I set right nought :
I am Robin Hood of Barnèsdale,
    Whom thou so long hast sought.

He that had neither been kith nor kin,
    Might have seen a full fair sight,
To see how together these yeomen went
    With blades both brown and bright.

To see how these yeomen together they fought
    Two hours of a summer's day :
Yet neither Robin Hood nor sir Guy
    Them fettled to fly away.

* Lime.

ROBIN HOOD AND GUY OF GISBORNE

Robin was reachles* of a root,
 And stumbled at that tide ;
And Guy was quick and nimble withal,
 And hit him o'er the left side.

Ah dear Lady, said Robin Hood, thou,
 Thou art both mother and may',†
I think it was never man's destiny
 To die before his day.

Robin thought on our Lady dear,
 And soon leapt up again,
And straight he came with a backward stroke,
 And he sir Guy hath slain.

He took sir Guy's head by the hair,
 And stuck it upon his bow's-end :
Thou hast been a traitor all thy life,
 Which thing must have an end.

Robin pull'd forth an Irish knife,
 And nick'd sir Guy in the face,
That he was never o' woman born,
 Could tell whose head it was.

   * Careless.   † Maid.

Says, Lie there, lie there now, sir Guy,
   And with me be not wroth;
If thou have had the worst strokes at my hand,
   Thou shalt have the better cloth.

Robin did off his gown of green,
   And on sir Guy did throw,
And he put on that capull hide,
   That clad him top to toe.

The bow, the arrows, and little horn,
   Now with me I will bear;
For I will away to Barnèsdale,
   To see how my men do fare.

Robin Hood set Guy's horn to his mouth,
   And a loud blast in it did blow,
That beheard the sheriff of Nottingham,
   As he leaned under a lowe.*

Hearken, hearken, said the sheriff,
   I hear now tidings good,
For yonder I hear sir Guy's horn blow,
   And he hath slain Robin Hood.

            * Little hill.

Yonder I hear sir Guy's horn blow,
  It blows so well in tide,
And yonder comes that wighty yeoman,
  Clad in his capull hide.

Come hither, come hither, thou good sir Guy,
  Ask what thou wilt of me.
O I will none of thy gold, said Robin,
  Nor I will none of thy fee.

But now I have slain the master, he says,
  Let me go strike the knave ;
For this is all the reward I ask ;
  Nor no other will I have.

Thou art a madman, said the sheriff,
  Thou should'st have had a knight's fee :
But seeing thy asking hath been so bad,
  Well granted it shall be.

When Little John heard his master speak,
  Well knew he it was his steven :*
Now shall I be loosed, quoth Little John,
  With Christe his might in heaven.

* Voice.

Fast Robin he hied him to Little John,
   He thought to loose him belive ;*
The sheriff and all his company
   Fast after him did drive.

Stand back, stand back, said Robin ;
   Why draw you me so near ?
It was never the use in our country,
   One's shrift another should hear.

But Robin pull'd forth an Irish knife,
   And loosed John hand and foot,
And gave him sir Guy's bow into his hand,
   And bade it be his boote.

Then John he took Guy's bow in his hand,
   His bolts and arrows each one :
When the sheriff saw Little John bend his bow,
   He fettled him to be gone.

Towards his house in Nottingham town,
   He fled full fast away ;
And so did all the company :
   Not one behind would stay.

* Immediately.

But he could neither run so fast,
  Nor away so fast could ride,
But Little John with an arrow so broad,
  He shot him into the back-side.

THE CHILDE* OF ELLE.

N yonder hill a castle stands,
    With walls and towers bedight,†
And yonder lives the Childe of Elle,
    A young and comely knight.

The Childe of Elle to his garden went,
    And stood at his garden-pale,
When, lo! he beheld fair Emmeline's page
    Come tripping down the dale.

The Childe of Elle he hied him thence,
    I wist he stood not still,
And soon he met fair Emmeline's page
    Come climbing up the hill.

    * Knight.   † Bedeck'd.

Now Christe thee save, thou little foot-page,
  Now Christe thee save and see!
Oh tell me how does thy lady gay,
  And what may thy tidings be?

My lady she is all woe-begone,
  And the tears they fall from her eyne;*
And aye she laments the deadly feud
  Between her house and thine.

And here she sends thee a silken scarf
  Bedewed with many a tear,
And bids thee sometimes think on her,
  Who lovèd thee so dear.

And here she sends thee a ring of gold,
  The last boon thou may'st have,
And bids thee wear it for her sake,
  When she is laid in grave.

For, ah! her gentle heart is broke,
  And in grave soon must she be,
For her father hath chose her a new new love,
  And forbid her to think of thee.

* Eyes.

Her father hath brought her a carlish* knight,
    Sir John of the north countrey,
And within three days she must him wed,
    Or he vows he will her slay.

Now hie thee back, thou little foot-page,
    And greet thy lady from me,
And tell her that I, her own true love,
    Will die, or set her free.

Now hie thee back, thou little foot-page,
    And let thy fair lady know,
This night will I be at her bower-window,
    Betide me weal or woe.

The boy he tripped, the boy he ran,
    He neither stint† nor stay'd
Until he came to fair Emmeline's bower,
    When, kneeling down, he said,

O lady, I've been with thine own true love,
    And he greets thee well by me;
This night will he be at thy bower-window,
    And die or set thee free.

        * Churlish.   † Stopped.

Now day was gone, and night was come,
　And all were fast asleep,
All save the lady Emmeline,
　Who sate in her bower to weep:

And soon she heard her true loves voice
　Low whispering at the wall;
Awake, awake, my dear lady,
　'Tis I, thy true love, call.

Awake, awake, my lady dear,
　Come, mount this fair palfrey:
This ladder of ropes will let thee down,
　I'll carry thee hence away.

Now nay, now nay, thou gentle knight,
　Now nay, this may not be;
For aye should I tint* my maiden fame,
　If alone I should wend† with thee.

O lady, thou with a knight so true
　May'st safely wend alone;
To my lady mother I will thee bring,
　Where marriage shall make us one.

* Lose.　　　　† Go.

My father he is a baron bold,
  Of lineage proud and high ;
And what would he say if his daughter
  Away with a knight should fly?

Ah ! well I wot, he never would rest,
  Nor his meat should do him no good,
Till he had slain thee, Childe of Elle,
  And seen thy dear heart's blood.

O lady, wert thou in thy saddle set,
  And a little space him fro',
I would not care for thy cruel father,
  Nor the worst that he could do.

O lady, wert thou in thy saddle set,
  And once without this wall,
I would not care for thy cruel father,
  Nor the worst that might befall.

Fair Emmeline sighed, fair Emmeline wept,
  And aye her heart was woe :
At length he seized her lily-white hand,
  And down the ladder he drew :

And thrice he clasped her to his breast,
　And kissed her tenderly :
The tears that fell from her fair eyes,
　Ran like the fountain free.

He mounted himself on his steed so tall,
　And her on a fair palfrey,
And slung his bugle about his neck,
　And roundly they rode away.

All this beheard her own damsel,
　In her bed wherein she lay ;
Quoth she, My lord shall know of this,
　So I shall have gold and fee.

Awake, awake, thou baron bold !
　Awake, my noble dame !
Your daughter is fled with the Childe of Elle,
　To do the deed of shame.

The baron he woke, the baron he rose,
　And called his merry men all :
And come thou forth, Sir John the knight,
　Thy lady is carried to thrall.

Fair Emmeline scarce had ridden a mile,
  A mile forth of the town,
When she was aware of her father's men
  Come galloping over the down :

And foremost came the carlish knight,
  Sir John of the north countrey :
Now stop, now stop, thou false traitor,
  Nor carry that lady away.

For she is come of high lineage,
  And was of a lady born,
And ill it beseems thee, a false churl's son,
  To carry her hence to scorn.

Now loud thou liest, Sir John the knight,
  Now thou dost lie of me ;
A knight me got, and a lady me bore,
  So never did none by thee.

But light now down, my lady fair,
  Light down, and hold my steed,
While I and this discourteous knight
  Do try this arduous deed.

The Childe of Elle.

But light now down, my dear lady,
  Light down, and hold my horse ;
While I and this discourteous knight
  Do try our valour's force.

Fair Emmeline sighed, fair Emmeline
  And aye her heart was woe,
While 'twixt her love and the carlish knight
  Past many a baleful blow.

The Childe of Elle he fought so well,
  As his weapon he waved amain,
That soon he had slain the carlish knight,
  And laid him upon the plain.

And now the baron and all his men
  Full fast approached nigh :
Ah ! what may lady Emmeline do !
  'Twere now no boote* to fly.

Her lover he put his horn to his mouth,
  And blew both loud and shrill,
And soon he saw his own merry men
  Come riding over the hill.

* Good.

Now hold thy hand, thou bold baròn,
  I pray thee, hold thy hand,
Nor ruthless rend two gentle hearts,
  Fast knit in true love's band.

Thy daughter I have dearly loved
  Full long and many a day;
But with such love as holy kirk
  Hath freely said we may.

O give consent she may be mine,
  And bless a faithful pair:
My lands and livings are not small,
  My house and lineage fair:

My mother she was an earl's daughter,
  And a noble knight my sire—
The baron he frowned, and turned away
  With mickle* dole and ire.

Fair Emmeline sighed, fair Emmeline wept,
  And did all trembling stand:
At length she sprang upon her knee,
  And held his lifted hand.

                    * Much grief.

THE CHILDE OF ELLE

Pardon, my lord and father dear,
  This fair young knight and me :
Trust me, but for the carlish knight,
  I never had fled from thee.

Oft have you called your Emmeline
  Your darling and your joy ;
O let not then your harsh resolves
  Your Emmeline destroy.

The baron he stroked his dark-brown cheek,
  And turned his head aside
To wipe away the starting tear
  He proudly strove to hide.

In deep revolving thought he stood,
  And mused a little space :
Then raised fair Emmeline from the ground,
  With many a fond embrace.

Here, take her, Childe of Elle, he said,
  And gave her lily hand ;
Here, take my dear and only child,
  And with her half my land :

Thy father once mine honour wronged
  In days of youthful pride ;
Do thou the injury repair
  In fondness for thy bride.

And as thou love her, and hold her dear,
  Heaven prosper thee and thine :
And now my blessing wend wi' thee,
  My lovely Emmeline.

ADAM BELL, CLYM OF THE CLOUGH,* AND WILLIAM OF CLOUDESLY.

PART THE FIRST.

ERRY it was in the green forèst
   Among the leavès green,
   Wherein men hunt east and west
   With bows and arrows keen;

To raise the deer out of their den;
   Such sights hath oft been seen;
As by three yeomen of the north countrèy,
   By them it is I mean.

The one of them hight† Adam Bell,
   The other Clym of the Clough,
The third was William of Cloudesly,
   An archer good enough.

---

* Clem (Clement) of the cliff.   † Called.

They were outlawed for venison,
　　These yeomen everyone ;
They swore together upon a day,
　　To English wood to be gone.

Now lithe and listen, gentlemen,
　　That of mirth loveth to hear :
Two of them were single men,
　　The third had a wedded fere.*

William was the wedded man,
　　Much more then was his care :
He said to his brethren upon a day,
　　To Carlisle he would fare,†

For to speak with fair Alice his wife,
　　And with his children three.
By my troth, said Adam Bell,
　　Not by the counsel of me :

For if ye go to Carlisle, brother,
　　And from this wild wood wend,
If that the justice should you take,
　　Your life were at an end.

* Mate.　　　　　　† Pass.

If that I come not to-morrow, brother,
  By pryme* to you again,
Trust you then that I am taken
  Or else that I am slain.

He took his leave of his brethren two,
  And to Carlisle he is gone :
There he knock'd at his own window
  Shortly and anon.

Where be you, fair Alice, he said,
  My wife and children three ?
Lightly let in thine own husbànd,
  William of Cloudesly.

Alas ! then said fair Alice,
  And sighed wondrous sore,
This place hath been beset for you
  This half a year and more.

Now am I here, said Cloudesly,
  I would that in I were :
Now fetch us meat and drink enough,
  And let us make good cheer.

She fetched him meat and drink plenty,
　Like a true wedded wife;
And pleased him with that she had,
　Whom she loved as her life.

There lay an old wife in that place,
　A little beside the fire,
Which William had found of charity
　More than seven year.

Up she rose, and forth she goes,
　Evil may she speed therefore;
For she had set no foot on ground
　In seven year before.

She went unto the justice hall,
　As fast as she could hie:
This night, she said, is come to town
　William of Cloudesly.

Thereat the justice was full fayne,*
　And so was the sheriff also:
Thou shalt not travel hither, dame, for nought;
　Thy meed thou shalt have ere thou go.

* Glad.

They gave to her a right good gown
    Of scarlet, and of grain :*
She took the gift, and home she went,
    And couched her down again.

They raised the town of merry Carlisle
    In all the haste they can ;
And came thronging to William's house,
    As fast as they might ran.

There they beset that good yeomàn
    Round about on every side :
William heard great noise of folks
    That thither-ward fast hied.

Alice opened a back windòw
    And looked all about,
She was 'ware of the justice and sheriff both,
    And with them a great rout.

Alas ! treason, cried Alice,
    Ever woe may thou be !
Go into my chamber, husband, she said,
    Sweet William of Cloudesly.

* Red.

He took his sword and his buckler,
   His bow and his children three,
And went into his strongest chamber,
   Where he thought surest to be.

Fair Alice, like a lover true,
   Took a pollaxe in her hand :
Said, He shall die that cometh in
   This door, while I may stand.

Cloudesly bent a right good bow,
   That was of a trusty tree,
He smote the justice on the breast,
   That his arrow burst in three.

A curse on his heart, said William,
   This day thy coat put on !
If it had been no better than mine,
   That had gone near thy bone.

Yield thee, Cloudesly, said the justice,
   And thy bow and thy arrows thee fro'.
A curse on his heart, said fair Alice,
   That my husband counselleth so.

WILLIAM OF CLOUDESLY

Set fire on the house, said the sheriff,
  Since it will no better be,
And burn we therein William, he said,
  His wife and children three.

They fired the house in many a place,
  The fire flew up on high :
Alas ! then cried fair Alice,
  I see we here shall die.

William opened a back window,
  That was in his chamber hi',
And there with sheets he did let down
  His wife and children three.

Have you here my treasure, said William,
  My wife and my children three :
For Christ's love do them no harm,
  But wreak you all on me.

William shot so wondrous well,
  Till his arrows were all ago',
And the fire so fast upon him fell
  That his bowstring burnt in two.

The sparkles burnt and fell upon
    Good William of Cloudesly :
Then was he a woeful man, and said,
    This is a coward's death to me.

Liever had I, said William,
    With my sword in the route to run,
Than here among mine enemies wode*
    Thus cruelly to burn.

He took his sword and his buckler,
    And among them all he ran,
Where the people were most in prece,†
    He smote down many a man.

There might no man abide his strokes,
    So fiercely on them he ran :
Then they threw windows, and doors on him,
    And so took that good yeomàn.

There they him bound both hand and foot,
    And in deep dungeon him cast :
Now Cloudesly, said the justice,
    Thou shalt be hanged in haste.

        * Wild.   † Pressed.

A pair of new gallows, said the sheriff,
  Now shall I for thee make ;
And the gates of Carlisle shall be shut :
  No man shall come in thereat.

Then shall not help Clym of the Clough,
  Nor yet shall Adam Bell,
Though they came with a thousand more,
  Nor all the devils in hell.

Early in the morning the justice uprose,
  To the gates first gan he to gon',
And commanded to be shut full close
  Lightly every one.

Then went he to the market place,
  As fast as he could hie ;
There a pair of new gallows he set up
  Beside the pillory.

A little boy among them asked,
  What meaneth that gallows-tree ?
They said to hang a good yeoman,
  Called William of Cloudesly.

That little boy was the town swine-herd,
    And kept fair Alice's swine;
Oft he had seen William in the wood,
    And given him there to dine.

He went out at a crevice in the wall,
    And lightly to the wood did gon';
There met he with these wight yeomen
    Shortly and anon.

Alas! then said that little boy,
    Ye tarry here all too long;
Cloudesly is taken, and dampned * to death,
    All ready for to hong.†

Alas! then said good Adam Bell,
    That ever we see this day!
He had better with us have tarried,
    So oft as we did him pray.

He might have dwelt in green forest,
    Under the shadows green,
And have kept both him and us at rest,
    Out of all trouble and teen.‡

---

* Condemned.   † Hang.   ‡ Sorrow.

Adam bent a right good bow,
  A great hart soon he had slain ;
Take that, child, he said, to thy dinner,
  And bring me mine arrow again.

Now go we hence, said these wight yeomen,
  Tarry we no longer here ;
We shall him borrow* by God his grace,
  Though we buy it full dear.

To Carlisle went these bold yeomen,
  All in the morning of May.
Here is a FYT† of Cloudesly,
  And another is for to say.

    * Redeem.   † Part of a song.

PART THE SECOND.

AND when they came to merry Carlisle,
All in the morning tide,
They found the gates shut them against
About on every side.

Alas! then said good Adam Bell,
That ever we were made men!
These gates be shut so wondrous fast,
We may not come therein.

Then bespake him Clym of the Clough,
With a wile we will us in bring;
Let us say we be messengers,
Straight come now from our king.

Adam said, I have a letter written,
  Now let us wisely work,
We will say we have the king's seal;
  I hold the porter no clerk.

Then Adam Bell beat on the gates
  With strokes great and strong,
The porter marvelled who was there,
  And to the gates he throng.*

Who is there now, said the porter,
  That maketh all this knocking?
We be two messengers, quoth Clym of the Clough,
  Be come right from our king.

We have a letter, said Adam Bell,
  To the justice we must it bring;
Let us in our message to do,
  That we may again to the king.

Here cometh none in, said the porter,
  By him that died on a tree,
Till a false thief be hanged up,
  Called William of Cloudesley.

        * Hastened.

Then spake the good yeoman Clym of the Clough,
    And swore by Mary free,
And if that we stand long without,
    Like a thief hanged thou shalt be.

Lo! here we have the king's seal :
    What, Lurden,* art thou wood?†
The porter thought it had been so,
    And lightly did off his hood.

Welcome is my lord's seal, he said ;
    For that ye shall come in.
He opened the gate full shortly ;
    An evil opening for him.

Now are we in, said Adam Bell,
    Whereof we are full fain ;
But Christ he knowes, that harrowed hell,
    How we shall come out again.

Had we the keys, said Clym of the Clough,
    Right well then should we speed,
Then might we come out well enough
    When we see time and need.

* Sluggard.   † Mad.

They called the porter to counsel,
  And wrung his neck in two,
And cast him in a deep dungeon,
  And took his keys him fro'.

Now am I porter, said Adam Bell,
  See, brother, the keys are here,
The worst porter to merry Carlisle
  That they had this hundred year.

And now will we our bows bend,
  Into the town will we go,
For to deliver our dear brother,
  That lyeth in care and woe.

Then they bent their good yew bows,
  And looked their strings were round,
The market place in merry Carlisle
  They beset that stound.*

And, as they looked them beside,
  A pair of new gallows they see,
And the justice with a quest of squires,
  Had judged William hanged to be.

  * Time.

And Cloudesly lay ready there in a cart,
  Fast bound both foot and hand ;
And a strong rope about his neck,
  All ready for to hang.

The justice called to him a lad,
  Cloudesly's clothes he should have,
To take the measure of that yeoman,
  Thereafter to make his grave.

I have seen as great marvel, said Cloudesly,
  As between this and pryme,*
He that maketh a grave for me
  Himself may lie therein.

Thou speakest proudly, said the justice,
  I will thee hang with my hand.
Full well heard this his brethren two,
  There still as they did stand.

Then Cloudesly cast his eyes aside,
  And saw his brethren twain
At a corner of the market place,
  Ready the justice for to slain.

* Noon.

I see comfort, said Cloudesly,
  Yet hope I well to fare,
If I might have my hands at will
  Right little would I care.

Then spake good Adam Bell
  To Clym of the Clough so free,
Brother, see you mark the justice well ;
  Lo ! yonder you may him see :

And at the sheriff shoot I will
  Strongly with arrow keen ;
A better shot in merry Carlisle
  This seven year was not seen.

They loosed their arrows both at once,
  Of no man had they dread ;
The one hit the justice, the other the sheriff,
  That both their sides 'gan bleed.

All men 'voided, that them stood nigh,
  When the justice fell to the ground,
And the sheriff nigh him by ;
  Either had his death's wound.

All the citizens fast began to fly,
　They durst no longer abide :
There lightly they loosed Cloudesly,
　Where he with ropes lay tied.

William start to an officer of the town,
　His axe from his hand he wrung,
On each side he smote them down,
　He thought he tarried too long.

William said to his brethren two,
　This day let us live and die,
If ever you have need, as I have now,
　The same shall you find by me.

They shot so well in that tide,
　Their strings were of silk full sure,
That they kept the streets on every side ;
　That battle did long endure.

They fought together as brethren true,
　Like hardy men and bold,
Many a man to the ground they threw,
　And many a heart made cold.

But when their arrows were all gone,
  Men pressed to them full fast,
They drew their swords then anon,
  And their bows from them cast.

They went lightly on their way,
  With swords and bucklers round ;
By that it was mid of the day,
  They made many a wound.

There was many an out-horn* in Carlisle blown,
  And the bells backward did ring,
Many a woman said, Alas !
  And many their hands did wring.

The mayor of Carlisle forth was come,
  With him a full great rout :
These yeomen dreaded him full sore,
  Of their lives they stood in doubt.

The mayor came armed at full great pace,
  With a pollaxe in his hand ;
Many a strong man with him was,
  There in that stowre† to stand.

---

  * Summons to arms.   * Fight.

The mayor smote at Cloudesly with his bill,
 His buckler he burst in two,
Full many a yeoman with great evil,
 Alas! Treason they cried for woe.
Keep well the gates fast, they bade,
 That these traitors thereout not go.

But all for nought was that they wrought,
 For so fast they down were laid,
Till they all three, that so manfully fought,
 Were gotten without, abroad.

Have here your keys, said Adam Bell,
 Mine office I here forsake,
And if you do by my counsel
 A new porter do ye make.

He threw their keys at their heads,
 And bade them well to thrive,
And all that letteth* any good yeoman
 To come and comfort his wife.

Thus be these good yeomen gone to the wood,
 And lightly, as leaf on lynde ;†

   * Hindereth.   † Lime-tree.

To laugh and be merry in their mood,
 Their enemies were far behind.

And when they came to English wood,
 Under the trusty tree,
There they found bows full good,
 And arrows full great plenty.

So God me help, said Adam Bell,
 And Clym of the Clough so free,
I would we were in merry Carlisle,
 Before that fair meynye.*

They sate them down, and made good cheer,
 And ate and drank full well.
A second FYT of the wighty yeomen,
 Another I will you tell.

* Company.

PART THE THIRD.

S they sat in the merry green wood,
 Under the green-wood tree,
They thought they heard a woman weep,
 But her they mought* not see.

Sore then sighed the fair Alice :
 That ever I saw this day !
For now is my dear husband slain :
 Alas ! and well-a-way !

Might I have spoken to his dear brethren,
 Or with either of them twain,
To show to them what him befell,
 My heart were out of pain.

   * Might for could.

Cloudesly walked a little beside,
    He looked under the green-wood lynde;
He was aware of his wife, and children three,
    Full woe in heart and mind.

Welcome, wife, then said William,
    Under this trusty tree:
I had ween'd yesterday, by sweet saint John,
    Thou shouldst me never have see'.

Now well is me that ye be here,
    My heart is out of woe;
Dame, he said, be merry and glad,
    And thank my brethren two.

Hereof to speak, said Adam Bell,
    I think it is no boot:
The meat, that we must sup withal,
    It runneth yet fast on foot.

Then went they down into a lawn,
    These noble archers all three;
Each of them slew a hart of grease,*
    The best that they could see.

* Fat hart.

Have here the best, Alice my wife,
  Said William of Cloudesly ;
Because ye so boldly stood by me
  When I was slain full nigh.

Then went they all into supper
  With such meat as they had ;
And thanked God of their fortune :
  They were both merry and glad.

And when they all had supped well,
  Certainly without lease,*
Cloudesly said, We will to our king,
  To get us a charter of peace.

Alice shall be at our sojourning
  In a nunnery here beside ;
My two sons shall with her go,
  And there they shall abide.

Mine eldest son shall go with me ;
  For him have you no care :
And he shall bring you word again,
  How that we do fare.

* Lies.

Thus be these yeomen to London gone,
  As fast as they might hie,
Till they came to the king's palace,
  Where they would needs be.

And when they came to the king's court,
  Unto the palace gate,
Of no man would they ask no leave,
  But boldly went in thereat.

They pressed prestly* into the hall,
  Of no man had they dread :
The porter came after, and did them call,
  And with them began to chide.

The usher said, Yeomen, what would ye have ?
  I pray you tell to me :
You might thus make officers shent :†
  Good sirs, of whence be ye ?

Sir, we be outlaws of the forest
  Certainly without lease ;
And hither we be come to our king,
  To get us a charter of peace.

----

    * Quickly.   * Disgraced.

And when they came before the king,
  As it was the law of the land,
They kneeled down without hindrance,
  And each held up his hand.

They said, Lord, we beseech thee here,
  That you will grant us grace ;
For we have slain your fat fallow deer
  In many a sundry place.

What be your names, then said our king,
  Anon that you tell me ?
They said, Adam Bell, Clym of the Clough,
  And William of Cloudesly.

Be ye those thieves, then said our king,
  That men have told of to me ?
Here to God I make a vow,
  Ye shall be hanged all three.

Ye shall be dead without mercy,
  As I am king of this land.
He commanded his officers everyone,
  Fast on them to lay hand.

ADAM BELL AND CLYM OF THE CLOUGH

There they took these good yeomen,
    And arrested them all three :
So may I thrive, said Adam Bell,
    This game liketh not me.

But, good lord, we beseech you now,
    That ye grant us grace,
Insomuch as freely to you we come,
    As freely we may from you pass,

With such weapons, as we have here,
    Till we be out of your place ;
And if we live this hundred year,
    We will ask you no grace.

Ye speak proudly, said the king;
    Ye shall be hanged all three.
That were great pity, then said the queen,
    If any grace might be.

My lord, when I came first into this land
    To be your wedded wife,
The first boon that I would ask,
    Ye would grant it me belyfe :*

* Immediately.

E 2

And I never asked none till now;
  Therefore, good lord, grant it me.
Now ask it, madam, said the king,
  And granted it shall be.

Then, good my lord, I you beseech,
  These yeomen grant ye me.
Madame, ye might have asked a boon,
  That should have been worth them all three.

Ye might have asked towers, and towns,
  Parks and forests plenty.
None so pleasant to my liking, she said ;
  Nor none so lefe* to me.

Madame, since it is your desire,
  Your asking granted shall be ;
But I had lever† have given you
  Good market towns three.

The queen she was a glad woman,
  And said, Lord, gramarcy :
I dare undertake for them,
  That true men shall they be.

            * Dear.   † Rather.

But good my lord, speak some merry word,
   That comfort they may see.
I grant you grace, then said our king :
   Wash, fellows, and to meat go ye.

They had not setten but a while
   Certain, without lesynge,*
There came messengers out of the north
   With letters to our king.

And when they came before the king,
   They knelt down on their knee :
And said, Lord, your officers greet you well,
   Of Carlisle in the north country.

How fareth my justice, said the king,
   And my sheriff also ?
Sir, they be slain, without leasynge,
   And many an officer mo'.

Who hath them slain, said the king ;
   Anon thou tell to me ?
Adam Bell, and Clym of the Clough,
   And William of Cloudesly.

* Lies.

Alas for ruth! then said our king:
  My heart is wondrous sore;
I had rather than a thousand pound,
  I had known of this before;

For I have granted them grace,
  And that forthinketh me:
But had I known all this before,
  They had been hanged all three.

The king he opened the letter anon,
  Himself he read it thro',
And found how these outlaws had slain
  Three hundred men and mo':

First the justice, and the sheriff,
  And the mayor of Carlisle town;
Of all the constables and catchpolls
  Alive were scarce left one:

The baillies, and the beadles both,
  And the sergeants of the law,
And forty foresters of the fee,*
  These outlaws had yslaw

* The King's foresters.   † Slain.

And broke his parks, and slain his deer;
Of all they chose the best;
Such perilous outlaws, as they were,
Walked not by east nor west.

When the king this letter had read,
In his heart he sighed sore:
Take up the tables anon he said,
For I may eat no more.

The king called his best archers
To the butts with him to go:
I will see these fellows shoot, he said,
In the north have wrought this woe.

The king's bowmen buske* them blyve,†
And the queen's archers also;
So did these three wighty yeomen;
With them they thought to go.

There twice or thrice they shot about
For to assay their hand;
There was no shot these yeomen shot,
That any prick might stand.

' Dress. † Instantly.

Then spake William of Cloudesly;
 By Him that for me died,
I hold him never no good archer,
 That shooteth at butts so wide.

At what a butt now would you shoot,
 I pray thee tell to me?
At such a butt, sir, he said,
 As men use in my country.

William went into a field,
 And with him his two brethren:
There they set up two hazel rods
 Twenty score paces between.

I hold him an archer, said Cloudesly,
 That yonder wand cleaveth in two.
Here is none such, said the king,
 Nor none that can so do.

I shall assay, sir, said Cloudesly,
 Or that I farther go.
Cloudesly with a bearyng* arrow
 Clave the wand in two.

    * An arrow that flies well.

Thou art the best archer, then said the king,
   For sooth that ever I see.
And yet for your love, said William,
   I will do more mastery.

I have a son is seven year old,
   He is to me full dear ;
I will him tie to a stake ;
   All shall see, that be here ;

And lay an apple upon his head,
   And go six score pace him fro',
And I myself with a broad arrow
   Shall cleave the apple in two.

Now haste thee, then said the king,
   By Him that died on a tree,
But if thou do not, as thou hast said,
   Hanged shalt thou be.

An thou touch his head or gown,
   In sight that men may see,
By all the saints that be in heaven,
   I shall hang you all three.

That I have promised, said William,
　That I will never forsake.
And there even before the king
　In the earth he drove a stake :

And bound thereto his eldest son,
　And bade him stand still thereat ;
And turned the child's face him from,
　Because he should not start.

An apple upon his head he set,
　And then his bow he bent :
Six score paces they were meaten,*
　And thither Cloudesly went.

There he drew out a fair broad arrow,
　His bow was great and long,
He set that arrow in his bow,
　That was both stiff and strong.

He prayed the people that were there,
　That they all still would stand,
For he that shooteth for such a wager,
　Behoveth a stedfast hand.

* Measured.

Much people prayed for Cloudesly,
   That his life saved might be,
And when he made him ready to shoot,
   There was many weeping ee.

But Cloudesly cleft the apple in two,
   His son he did not nee.*
Over Gods forbode,† said the king,
   That thou should shoot at me.

I give thee eighteen pence a day,
   And my bow shalt thou bear,
And over all the north country
   I make thee chief ranger.

And I thirteen pence a day, said the queen,
   By God, and by my fa';
Come fetch thy payment when thou wilt,
   No man shall say thee nay.

William, I make thee a gentleman
   Of clothing, and of fee :
And thy two brethren, yeomen of my chamber,
   For they are so seemly to see.

* Nigh.   † God forbid.

Your son, for he is tender of age,
  Of my wine-cellar he shall be ;
And when he cometh to man's estate,
  Better advanced shall be he.

And, William, bring to me your wife, said the queen,
  Me longeth her sore to see :
She shall be my chief gentlewoman,
  To govern my nursery.

The yeomen thanked them courteously.
  To some bishop will we wend,
Of all the sins, that we have done,
  To be assoyld* at his hand.

So forth be gone these good yeomen,
  As fast as they might he ;†
And after came and dwelled with the king,
  And died good men all three.

Thus ended the lives of these good yeomen ;
  God send them eternal bliss.
And all, that with a hand-bow shooteth,
  That of heaven they never miss.   Amen.

          * Absolved.   † Hie.

SIR LANCELOT DU LAKE.

WHEN Arthur first in court began,
    And was approved king,
By force of arms great victories won,
    And conquest home did bring.

Then into England straight he came
    With fifty good and able
Knights, that resorted unto him,
    And were of his round table :

And he had jousts and tournaments,
    Whereto were many prest,
Wherein some knights did far excell
    And far surmount the rest.

But one, Sir Lancelot du Lake,
  Who was approved well,
He for his deeds and feats of arms,
  All others did excell.

When he had rested him a while,
  In play, and game, and sport,
He said he would go prove himself
  In some adventurous sort.

He armed rode in forest wide,
  And met a damsel fair,
Who told him of adventures great,
  Whereto he gave good ear.

Such would I find, quoth Lancelot:
  For that cause came I hither.
Thou seem'st, quoth she, a knight full good,
  And I will bring thee thither,

Whereas a mighty knight doth dwell,
  That now is of great fame:
Therefore tell me what wight thou art,
  And what may be thy name.

SIR LANCELOT DU LAKE

My name is Lancelot du Lake.
　　Quoth she, it likes me then :
Here dwells a knight who never was
　　Yet matcht with any man :

Who has in prison threescore knights
　　And four, that he did wound ;
Knights of king Arthur's court they be,
　　And of his table round.

She brought him to a river side,
　　And also to a tree,
Whereon a copper bason hung,
　　And many shields to see.

He struck so hard, the bason broke ;
　　And Tarquin soon he spied :
Who drove a horse before him fast,
　　Whereon a knight lay tied.

Sir knight, then said Sir Lancelot,
　　Bring me that horse-load hither,
And lay him down, and let him rest ;
　　We'll try our force together :

For, as I understand, thou hast,
   So far as thou art able,
Done great despite and shame unto
   The knights of the Round Table.

If thou be of the Table Round,
   Quoth Tarquin speedily,
Both thee and all thy fellowship
   I utterly defy.

That's over much, quoth Lancelot, though,
   Defend thee by and by.
They set their spears unto their steeds,
   And each at other fly.

They couched their spears, (their horses ran,
   As though there had been thunder)
And struck them each immidst their shields,
   Wherewith they broke in sunder.

Their horses' backs brake under them,
   The knights were both astound :
To avoid their horses they make haste
   And light upon the ground.

They took them to their shields full fast,
  Their swords they drew out then,
With mighty strokes most eagerly
  Each at the other ran.

They wounded were, and bled full sore,
  For both for breath did stand,
And leaning on their swords awhile,
  Quoth Tarquin, Hold thy hand,

And tell to me what I shall ask.
  Say on, quoth Lancelot tho.*
Thou art, quoth Tarquin, the best knight
  That ever I did know;

And like a knight, that I did hate :
  So that thou be not he,
I will deliver all the rest,
  And eke accord with thee.

That is well said, quoth Lancelot;
  But since it must be so,
What knight is that thou hatest thus ?
  I pray thee to me show.

---

* Then.

F

His name is Lancelot du Lake,
   He slew my brother dear;
Him I suspect of all the rest:
   I would I had him here.

Thy wish thou hast, but yet unknown,
   I am Lancelot du Lake,
Now knight of Arthur's Table Round;
   King Haud's son, of Schuwake;

And I desire thee do thy worst.
   Ho, ho, quoth Tarquin tho,
One of us two shall end our lives
   Before that we do go.

If thou be Lancelot du Lake,
   Then welcome shalt thou be;
Wherefore see thou thyself defend,
   For now defy I thee.

They buckled then together so,
   Like unto wild boars rashing,*
And with their swords and shields they ran
   At one another slashing:

* Tearing.

The ground besprinkled was with blood :
  Tarquin began to yield ;
For he gave back for weariness,
  And low did bear his shield.

This soon Sir Lancelot espied,
  He leapt upon him then,
He pull'd him down upon his knee,
  And rushing* off his helm,

Forthwith he struck his neck in two,
  And, when he had so done,
From prison threescore knights and four
  Delivered every one.

* Tearing.

THE FROLICKSOME DUKE, OR THE TINKER'S
GOOD FORTUNE.

NOW as fame does report, a young duke keeps a
court,
One that pleases his fancy with frolicksome sport :
But amongst all the rest, here is one I protest,
Which will make you to smile when you hear the true jest :
A poor tinker he found, lying drunk on the ground,
As secure in a sleep as if laid in a swound.

The duke said to his men, William, Richard, and Ben,
Take him home to my palace, we'll sport with him then.
O'er a horse he was laid, and with care soon convey'd
To the palace, altho' he was poorly array'd :
Then they stript off his clothes, both his shirt, shoes, and hose,
And they put him to bed for to take his repose.

Having pull'd off his shirt, which was all over dirt,
They did give him clean holland, this was no great hurt :
On a bed of soft down, like a lord of renown,
They did lay him to sleep the drink out of his crown.
In the morning when day, then admiring he lay,
For to see the rich chamber both gaudy and gay.

Now he lay something late, in his rich bed of state,
Till at last knights and squires, they on him did wait ;
And the chamberlain bare,* then did likewise declare,
He desir'd to know what apparel he'd wear :
The poor tinker amaz'd, on the gentleman gaz'd,
And admired † how he to this honour was rais'd.

Tho' he seem'd something mute, yet he chose a rich suit,
Which he straitways put on without longer dispute ;
With a star on his side, which the tinker oft ey'd,
And it seem'd for to swell him no little with pride ;
For he said to himself, Where is Joan my sweet wife ?
Sure she never did see me so fine in her life.

From a convenient place, the right duke his good grace
Did observe his behaviour in every case.

---

* Bare-headed.   † Wondered.

To a garden of state, on the tinker they wait,
Trumpet sounding before him : thought he, this is great :
Where an hour or two, pleasant walks he did view,
With commanders and squires in scarlet and blue.

A fine dinner was drest, both for him and his guests,
He was plac'd at the table above all the rest,
In a rich chair or bed, lin'd with fine crimson red,
With a rich golden canopy over his head :
As he sat at his meat, the music play'd sweet,
With the choicest of singing his joys to complete.

While the tinker did dine, he had plenty of wine,
Rich canary with sherry and tent superfine.
Like a right honest soul, faith, he took off his bowl,
Till at last he began for to tumble and roll
From his chair to the floor, where he sleeping did snore,
Being seven times drunker than ever before.

Then the duke did ordain, they should strip him amain,
And restore him his old leather garments again :
Twas a point next the worst, yet perform it they must,
And they carried him strait, where they found him at first ;

Then he slept all the night, as indeed well he might ;
But when he did waken, his joys took their flight.

For his glory to him so pleasant did seem,
That he thought it to be but a mere golden dream ;
Till at length he was brought to the duke, where he sought
For a pardon, as fearing he had set him at nought ;
But his highness he said, Thou'rt a jolly bold blade,
Such a frolic before I think never was play'd.

Then his highness bespoke him a new suit and cloak,
Which he gave for the sake of this frolicksome joke ;
Nay, and five hundred pound, with ten acres of ground,
Thou shalt never, said he, range the countries around,
Crying " old brass to mend," for I'll be thy good friend,
Nay, and Joan thy sweet wife shall my duchess attend.

Then the tinker reply'd, What! must Joan my sweet bride
Be a lady in chariots of pleasure to ride ?
Must we have gold and land ev'ry day at command ?
Then I shall be a squire I well understand :
Well I thank your good grace, and your love I embrace,
I was never before in so happy a case.

THE MORE MODERN BALLAD OF CHEVY CHASE.

GOD prosper long our noble king,
  Our lives and safeties all ;
A woful hunting once there did
  In Chevy-Chase befall ;

To drive the deer with hound and horn,
  Earl Percy took his way ;
The child may rue that is unborn
  The hunting of that day.

The stout Earl of Northumberland
  A vow to God did make,
His pleasure in the Scottish woods
  Three summer days to take ;

Ballad of Chevy Chase.

The chiefest harts in Chevy-Chase
    To kill and bear away.
These tidings to Earl Douglas came,
    In Scotland where he lay :

Who sent Earl Percy present word,
    He would prevent his sport.
The English earl, not fearing that,
    Did to the woods resort

With fifteen hundred bow-men bold ;
    All chosen men of might,
Who knew full well in time of need
    To aim their shafts aright.

The gallant greyhounds swiftly ran,
    To chase the fallow deer:
On Monday they began to hunt,
    Ere day-light did appear ;

And long before high noon they had
    An hundred fat bucks slain ;
Then having din'd, the drovers went
    To rouse the deer again.

The bow-men mustered on the hills,
　　Well able to endure ;
Their backsides all, with special care,
　　That day were guarded sure.

The hounds ran swiftly through the woods,
　　The nimble deer to take,
That with their cries the hills and dales
　　An echo shrill did make.

Lord Percy to the quarry went,
　　To view the slaughter'd deer ;
Quoth he, Earl Douglas promisèd
　　This day to meet me here :

But if I thought he would not come,
　　No longer would I stay.
With that, a brave young gentleman
　　Thus to the earl did say :

Lo, yonder doth Earl Douglas come,
　　His men in armour bright ;
Full twenty hundred Scottish spears
　　All marching in our sight ;

All men of pleasant Teviotdale,
  Fast by the river Tweed :
O cease your sport, Earl Percy said,
  And take your bows with speed :

And now with me, my countrymen,
  Your courage forth advance ;
For never was there champion yet
  In Scotland or in France,

That ever did on horseback come,
  But if my hap it were,
I durst encounter man for man,
  With him to break a spear.

Earl Douglas on his milk-white steed,
  Most like a baron bold,
Rode foremost of his company,
  Whose armour shone like gold.

Show me, said he, whose men you be,
  That hunt so boldly here,
hat, without my consent, do chase
  And kill my fallow-deer ?

The man that first did answer make,
  Was noble Percy he;
Who said, We list not to declare,
  Nor show whose men we be:

Yet will we spend our dearest blood,
  Thy chiefest harts to slay.
Then Douglas swore a solemn oath,
  And thus in rage did say,

Ere thus will I out-braved be,
  One of us two shall die:
I know thee well, an earl thou art;
  Lord Percy, so am I.

But trust me, Percy, pity 'twere,
  And great offence to kill
Any of these our guiltless men,
  For they have done no ill.

Let thou and I the battle try,
  And set our men aside.
Accurst be he, Earl Percy said,
  By whom this is denied.

Ballad of Chevy Chase.

Then stept a gallant squire forth,
　Witherington was his name,
Who said, I would not have it told
　To Henry our king for shame,

That e'er my captain fought on foot,
　And I stood looking on.
You be two earls, said Witherington,
　And I a squire alone :

I'll do the best that do I may,
　While I have power to stand :
While I have power to wield my sword,
　I'll fight with heart and hand.

Our English archers bent their bows,
　Their hearts were good and true ;
At the first flight of arrows sent,
　Full four-score Scots they slew.

Yet bides Earl Douglas on the bent.*
　As Chieftain stout and good,
As valiant Captain, all unmov'd
　The shock he firmly stood.

* Field.

His host he parted had in three,
  As leader ware and try'd,
And soon his spearmen on their foes
  Bore down on every side.

Throughout the English archery
  They dealt full many a wound :
But still our valiant Englishmen
  All firmly kept their ground :

And throwing straight their bows away,
  They grasp'd their swords so bright :
And now sharp blows, a heavy shower,
  On shields and helmets light.

They clos'd full fast on every side,
  No slackness there was found ;
And many a gallant gentleman
  Lay gasping on the ground.

O Christ ! it was a grief to see,
  And likewise for to hear,
The cries of men lying in their gore,
  And scattered here and there.

At last these two stout earls did meet,
  Like captains of great might:
Like lions wood,* they laid on loud,
  And made a cruel fight :

They fought until they both did sweat,
  With swords of tempered steel ;
Until the blood, like drops of rain,
  They trickling down did feel.

Yield thee, Lord Percy, Douglas said ;
  In faith I will thee bring,
Where thou shalt high advanced be
  By James our Scottish king :

Thy ransom I will freely give,
  And thus report of thee,
Thou art the most courageous knight,
  That ever I did see.

No, Douglas, quoth Earl Percy then,
  Thy proffer I do scorn ;
I will not yield to any Scot,
  That ever yet was born.

* Wild.

With that, there came an arrow keen
Out of an English bow,
Which struck Earl Douglas to the heart,
A deep and deadly blow:

Who never spake more words than these,
Fight on, my merry men all;
For why, my life is at an end;
Lord Percy sees my fall.

Then leaving life, Earl Percy took
The dead man by the hand;
And said, Earl Douglas, for thy life
Would I had lost my land.

O Christ! my very heart doth bleed
With sorrow for thy sake;
For sure, a more renowned knight
Mischance could never take.

A knight amongst the Scots there was,
Which saw Earl Douglas die,
Who straight in wrath did vow revenge
Upon the Lord Percy:

CHEVY CHASE

Sir Hugh Montgomery was he call'd
  Who, with a spear most bright,
Well-mounted on a gallant steed,
  Ran fiercely through the fight;

And past the English archers all,
  Without all dread or fear;
And through Earl Percy's body then
  He thrust his hateful spear;

With such a vehement force and might
  He did his body gore,
The staff went through the other side
  A large cloth-yard, and more.

So thus did both these nobles die,
  Whose courage none could stain;
An English archer then perceiv'd
  The noble earl was slain;

He had a bow bent in his hand,
  Made of a trusty tree;
An arrow of a cloth-yard long
  Up to the head drew he:

Against Sir Hugh Montgomery,
    So right the shaft he set,
The grey goose-wing that was thereon
    In his heart's blood was wet.

This fight did last from break of day
    Till setting of the sun ;
For when they rung the evening bell,*
    The battle scarce was done.

With brave Earl Percy, there was slain
    Sir John of Egerton,
Sir Robert Ratcliff, and Sir John,
    Sir James that bold Baròn :

And with Sir George and stout Sir James,
    Both knights of good account,
Good Sir Ralph Raby there was slain,
    Whose prowess did surmount.

For Witherington needs must I wail,
    As one in doleful dumps ;
For when his legs were smitten off,
    He fought upon his stumps.

                * The curfew.

And with Earl Douglas, there was slain
   Sir Hugh Montgomery,
Sir Charles Murray, that from the field
   One foot would never flee.

Sir Charles Murray, of Ratcliff, too,
   His sister's son was he ;
Sir David Lamb, so well esteem'd,
   Yet saved could not be.

And the Lord Maxwell in like case
   Did with Earl Douglas die :
Of twenty hundred Scottish spears,
   Scarce fifty-five did fly.

Of fifteen hundred Englishmen,
   Went home but fifty-three ;
The rest were slain in Chevy Chase,
   Under the greenwood tree.

Next day did many widows come,
   Their husbands to bewail ;
They washed their wounds in brinish tears,
   But all would not prevail.

Their bodies, bathed in purple gore,
  They bare with them away:
They kiss'd them dead a thousand times,
  Ere they were clad in clay.

This news was brought to Edinburgh,
  Where Scotland's king did reign,
That brave Earl Douglas suddenly
  Was with an arrow slain :

O heavy news, King James did say,
  Scotland can witness be,
I have not any captain more
  Of such account as he.

Like tidings to King Henry came,
  Within as short a space,
That Percy of Northumberland
  Was slain in Chevy Chase :

Now God be with him, said our king,
  Since it will no better be ;
I trust I have, within my realm,
  Five hundred as good as he :

Yet shall not Scots nor Scotland say,
　But I will vengeance take :
I'll be revenged on them all,
　For brave Earl Percy's sake.

This vow full well the king perform'd
　After, at Humbledown ;
In one day, fifty knights were slain,
　With lords of great renown :

And of the rest, of small account,
　Did many thousands die :
Thus endeth the hunting of Chevy Chase,
　Made by the Earl Percy.

God save our king, and bless this land
　In plenty, joy, and peace ;
And grant henceforth, that foul debate
　'Twixt noblemen may cease.

KING EDWARD IV. AND THE TANNER OF
TAMWORTH.

IN summer time, when leaves grow green,
 And blossoms bedeck the tree,
 King Edward would a hunting ride,
  Some pastime for to see.

With hawk and hound he made him bowne,*
 With horn, and eke with bow;
To Drayton Basset he took his way,
 With all his lords in a row.

And he had ridden o'er dale and down
 By eight of clock in the day,
When he was 'ware of a bold tannèr,
 Come riding along the way.

    * Ready.

A fair russet coat the tanner had on
 Fast buttoned under his chin,
And under him a good cow-hide,
 And a mare of four shilling.*

Now stand you still, my good lords all,
 Under the greenwood spray;
And I will wend to yonder fellow,
 To weet † what he will say.

God speed, God speed thee, said our king.
 Thou art welcome, sir, said he.
The readiest way to Drayton Basset
 I pray thee to show to me.

To Drayton Basset wouldst thou go,
 Fro' the place where thou dost stand?
The next pair of gallows thou comest unto,
 Turn in upon thy right hand.

That is an unready way, said our king,
 Thou dost but jest I see;
Now show me out the nearest way,
 And I pray thee wend with me.

---

* A shilling was a large sum in those days.   † Know.

Away with a vengeance ! quoth the tanner:
  I hold thee out of thy wit :
All day have I ridden on Brock my marc,
  And I am fasting yet.

Go with me down to Drayton Basset,
  No dainties we will spare ;
All day shalt thou eat and drink of the best,
  And I will pay thy fare.

Gramercy for nothing, the tanner replied,
  Thou payest no fare of mine :
I trow I've more nobles in my purse,
  Than thou hast pence in thine.

God give thee joy of them, said the king,
  And send them well to priefe.*
The tanner would fain have been away,
  For he weened he had been a thief.

What art thou, he said, thou fine fellòw,
  Of thee I am in great fear,
For the clothes, thou wearest upon thy back,
  Might beseem a lord to wear.

* Prove.

I never stole them, quoth our king,
    I tell you, sir, by the rood,
Then thou playest, as many an unthrift doth,
    And standest in midst of thy good.*

What tidings hear you, said the king,
    As you ride far and near?
I hear no tidings, sir, by the mass,
    But that cow-hides are dear.

Cow-hides! cow-hides! what things are those?
    I marvel what they be!
What art thou a fool? the tanner replied;
    I carry one under me.

What craftsman art thou? said the king,
    I pray thee tell me true.
I am a barker,† sir, by my trade;
    Now tell me what art thou?

I am a poor courtier, sir, quoth he,
    That am forth of service worn;
And fain I would thy prentice be,
    Thy cunning for to learn.

i.e. Hast no other wealth but what thou carriest about thee.
    † A dealer in bark.

Marry heaven forfend, the tanner replied,
  That thou my prentice were :
Thou wouldst spend more good than I should win
  By forty shilling a year.

Yet one thing would I, said our king,
  If thou wilt not seem strange :
Though my horse be better than thy mare,
  Yet with thee I fain would change.

Why if with me thou fain wilt change,
  As change full well may we,
By the faith of my body, thou proud fellow,
  I will have some boot of thee.

That were against reason, said the king,
  I swear, so mote I thee :*
My horse is better than thy mare,
  And that thou well mayst see.

Yea, sir, but Brock is gentle and mild,
  And softly she will fare :
Thy horse is unruly and wild, I wiss ;
  Aye skipping here and there.

* May I thrive.

What boot wilt thou have? our king replied;
  Now tell me in this stound.
No pence, nor halfpence, by my faith,
  But a noble in gold so round.

Here's twenty groats of white money,
  Sith thou will have it of me.
I would have sworn now, quoth the tanner,
  Thou hadst not had one penny.

But since we two have made a change,
  A change we must abide,
Although thou hast gotten Brock my mare,
  Thou gettest not my cow-hide.

I will not have it, said the king,
  I swear, so mote I thee;
Thy foul cow-hide I would not bear,
  If thou wouldst give it to me.

The tanner he took his good cow-hide,
  That of the cow was hilt;*
And threw it upon the king's saddle,
  That was so fairly gilt.

* Flayed.

Now help me up, thou fine fellow,
  'Tis time that I were gone ;
When I come home to Gyllian my wife,
  She'll say I am a gentleman.

When the tanner he was in the king's saddle,
  And his foot in the stirrup was ;
He marvelled greatly in his mind,
  Whether it were gold or brass.

But when his steed saw the cow's tail wag,
  And eke the black cow-horn ;
He stamped, and stared, and away he ran,
  As the devil had him borne.

The tanner he pulled, the tanner he sweat,
  And held by the pummel fast,
At length the tanner came tumbling down ;
  His neck he had well-nigh brast.*

Take thy horse again with a vengeance, he said,
  With me he shall not bide.
My horse would have borne thee well enough,
  But he knew not of thy cow-hide.

                    * Broken.

THE TANNER OF TAMWORTH

Yet if again thou fain wouldst change,
  As change full well may we,
By the faith of my body, thou jolly tannèr,
  I will have some boot of thee.

What boot wilt thou have, the tanner replied,
  Now tell me in this stound ? *
No pence nor half-pence, sir, by my faith,
  But I will have twenty pound.

Here's twenty groats out of my purse ;
  And twenty I have of thine :
And I have one more, which we will spend
  Together at the wine.

The king set a bugle horn to his mouth,
  And blew both loud and shrill :
And soon came lords, and soon came knights,
  Fast riding over the hill.

Now, out alas! the tanner he cried,
  That ever I saw this day!
Thou art a strong thief, yon come thy fellows
  Will bear my cow-hide away.

* Time.

They are no thieves, the king replied
    I swear, so mote I thee :
But they are the lords of the north country,
    Here come to hunt with me.

And soon before our king they came,
    And knelt down on the ground :
Then might the tanner have been away,
    He had lever* than twenty pound.

A collar, a collar, here : said the king,
    A collar he loud 'gan cry :
Then would he lever than twenty pound,
    He had not been so nigh.

A collar, a collar, the tanner he said,
    I trow it will breed sorrow :
After a collar cometh a halter,
    I trow I shall be hang'd to-morrow.

Be not afraid, tanner, said our king ;
    I tell thee, so mote I thee,
Lo here I make thee the best esquire
    That is in the north country.

        * Rather.

For Plumpton-park I will give thee,
　With tenements fair beside :
'Tis worth three hundred marks by the year,
　To maintain thy good cow-hide.

Gramercy, my liege, the tanner replied,
　For the favour thou hast me shown :
If ever thou comest to merry Tamworth,
　Neat's * leather shall clout thy shoen.†

* Cow's.　　　　† Mend thy shoes.

THE HEIR OF LINNE.

PART THE FIRST.

LITHE* and listen, gentlemen,
   To sing a song I will begin:
It is of a lord of fair Scotland,
   Which was the unthrifty heir of Linne.

His father was a right good lord,
   His mother a lady of high degree;
But they, alas! were dead, him fro',
   And he lov'd keeping company.

To spend the day with merry cheer,
   To drink and revel every night,
To card and dice from eve to morn,
   It was, I ween, his heart's delight.

* Attend.

To ride, to run, to rant, to roar,
  To alway spend and never spare,
I know, an' it were the king himself,
  Of gold and fee he might be bare.

So fares the unthrifty lord of Linne
  Till all his gold is gone and spent;
And he maun sell his lands so broad,
  His house, and lands, and all his rent.

His father had a keen stewàrd,
  And John o' the Scales was called he:
But John is become a gentleman,
  And John has got both gold and fee.

Says, Welcome, welcome, lord of Linne,
  Let nought disturb thy merry cheer;
If thou wilt sell thy lands so broad,
  Good store of gold I'll give thee here.

My gold is gone, my money is spent;
  My land now take it unto thee:
Give me the gold, good John o' the Scales,
  And thine for aye my land shall be.

H

Then John he did him to record draw,
  And John he cast him a gods-pennie;*
But for every pound that John agreed,
  The land, I wis, was well worth three.

He told him the gold upon the board,
  He was right glad his land to win;
The gold is thine, the land is mine,
  And now I'll be the lord of Linne.

Thus he hath sold his land so broad,
  Both hill and holt,† and moor and fen,
All but a poor and lonesome lodge,
  That stood far off in a lonely glen.

For so he to his father hight,‡
  My son, when I am gone, said he,
Then thou wilt spend thy land so broad,
  And thou wilt spend thy gold so free:

But swear me now upon the cross,
  That lonesome lodge thou'lt never spend;
For when all the world doth frown on thee,
  Thou there shalt find a faithful friend.

* Earnest-money.   † Wood.   ‡ Promised.

The heir of Linne is full of gold :
 And come with me, my friends, said he,
Let's drink, and rant, and merry make,
 And he that spares, ne'er mote he thee.*

They ranted, drank, and merry made,
 Till all his gold it waxed thin ;
And then his friends they slunk away;
 They left the unthrifty heir of Linne.

He had never a penny left in his purse,
 Never a penny left but three,
And one was brass, another was lead,
 And another it was white money.

Now well-a-day, said the heir of Linne,
 Now well-a-day, and woe is me,
For when I was the lord of Linne,
 I never wanted gold nor fee.

But many a trusty friend have I,
 And why should I feel grief or care ?
I'll borrow of them all by turns,
 So need I not be never bare.

* May he thrive.

H 2

But one, I wis, was not at home;
   Another had paid his gold away;
Another called him thriftless loon,
   And bade him sharply wend his way.

Now well-a-day, said the heir of Linne,
   Now well-a-day, and woe is me;
For when I had my lands so broad,
   On me they liv'd right merrily.

To beg my bread from door to door
   I wis, it were a burning shame:
To rob and steal it were a sin:
   To work my limbs I cannot frame.

Now I'll away to lonesome lodge,
   For there my father bade me wend;
When all the world should frown on me,
   I there should find a trusty friend.

THE HEIR OF LINNE.

AWAY then hied the heir of Linne
    O'er hill and holt, and moor and fen,
    Until he came to lonesome lodge,
    That stood so low in a lonely glen.

He looked up, he looked down,
    In hope some comfort for to win:
But bare and loathly were the walls.
    Here's sorry cheer, quo' the heir of Linne.

The little window dim and dark
    Was hung with ivy, brier, and yew;
No shimmering sun here ever shone;
    No wholesome breeze here ever blew.

No chair nor table he mote spy,
No cheerful hearth, no welcome bed,
Nought save a rope with running noose.
That dangling hung up o'er his head.

And over it in broad lettèrs,
These words were written plain to see:
" Ah ! graceless wretch, hast spent thine all,
And brought thyself to penury ?

" All this my boding mind misgave,
I therefore left this trusty friend :
Let it now shield thy foul disgrace,
And all thy shame and sorrows end."

Sorely shent * wi' this rebuke,
Sorely shent was the heir of Linne ;
His heart, I wis, was near to burst
With guilt and sorrow, shame and sin.

Never a word spake the heir of Linne,
Never a word he spake but three :
This is a trusty friend indeed,
And is right welcome unto me.

* Disgraced.

Then round his neck the cord he drew,
    And sprang aloft with his bodỳ :
When lo ! the ceiling burst in twain,
    And to the ground came tumbling he.

Astonished lay the heir of Linne,
    Nor knew if he were live or dead :
At length he looked, and saw a bill,*
    And in it a key of.gold so red.

He took the bill, and looked it on,
    Straight good comfort found he there :
It told him of a hole in the wall,
    In which there stood three chests in-fere.†

Two were full of the beaten gold,
    The third was full of white monèy ;
And over them in broad lettèrs
    These words were written so plain to see :

" Once more, my son, I set thee clear ;
    Amend thy life and follies past ;
For but thou amend thee of thy life,
    That rope must be thy end at last."

      * Writing.   † Together.

And let it be, said the heir of Linne ;
 And let it be, but* if I amend :
For here I will make my vow,
 This reade † shall guide me to the end.

Away then went with a merry cheer,
 Away then went the heir of Linne ;
I wis, he neither ceas'd nor blanne,‡
 Till John o' the Scales' house he did win.

And wncn he came to John o' the Scales,
 Up at the speere § then looked he ;
There sat three lords upon a row,
 Were drinking of the wine so free.

And John himself sat at the board-head,
 Because now lord of Linne was he.
I pray thee, he said, good John o' the Scales,
 One forty pence for to lend me.

Away, away, thou thriftless loon ;
 Away, away, this may not be ;
For Christ's curse on my head, he said,
 If ever I trust thee one pennie.

---

* Unless.   † Counsel   ‡ Lingered.   § Hole in the window.

Then bespake the heir of Linne,
  To John o' the Scales' wife then spake he:
Madame, some alms on me bestow,
  I pray for sweet saint Charity.

Away, away, thou thriftless loon,
  I swear thou gettest no alms of me;
For if we should hang any losel * here,
  The first we would begin with thee.

Then bespake a good fellow,
  Which sat at John o' the Scales his board;
Said, Turn again, thou heir of Linne;
  Some time thou wast a well good lord:

Some time a good fellow thou hast been,
  And sparedst not thy gold and fee;
Therefore I'll lend thee forty pence,
  And other forty if need be.

And ever, I pray thee, John o' the Scales,
  To let him sit in thy company:
For well I wot thou hadst his land,
  And a good bargain it was to thee.

* Worthless fellow.

Up then spake him John o' the Scales,
  All wood * he answer'd him again :
Now Christ's curse on my head, he said,
  But I did lose by that bargàin.

And here I proffer thee, heir of Linne,
  Before these lords so fair and free,
Thou shalt have it back again better cheap,
  By a hundred marks, than I had it of thee.

I draw you to record, lords, he said.
  With that he cast him a gods-pennie :
Now by my fay, said the heir of Linne,
  And here, good John, is thy monèy.

And he pull'd forth three bags of gold,
  And laid them down upon the board :
All woe begone was John o' the Scales,
  So shent † he could say never a word.

He told him forth the good red gold,
  He told it forth with mickle din.
The gold is thine, the land is mine,
  And now again I'm the lord of Linne.

* Wild.   † Disgraced.

Page 106

THE HEIR OF LINNE

Says, Have thou here, thou good fellow,
  Forty pence thou didst lend me :
Now I am again the lord of Linne,
  And forty pounds I will give thee.

I'll make thee keeper of my forest,
  Both of the wild deer and the tame ;
For but I reward thy bounteous heart,
  I wis, good fellow, I were to blame.

Now well-a-day ! saith Joan o' the Scales :
  Now well-a-day ! and woe is my life !
Yesterday I was lady of Linne,
  Now I'm but John o' the Scales his wife.

Now fare thee well, said the heir of Linne ;
  Farewell now, John o' the Scales, said he :
Christ's curse light on me, if ever again
  I bring my lands in jeopardy.

SIR ANDREW BARTON.

HEN Flora with her fragrant flowers
 Bedecked the earth so trim and gay,
 And Neptune with his dainty showers
  Came to present the month of May,'
King Henry rode to take the air,
 Over the river Thames past he;
When eighty merchànts of London came,
 And down they knelt upon their knee.

O ye are welcome, rich merchants;
 Good sailors, welcome unto me.
They swore by the rood, they were sailors good,
 But rich merchànts they could not be:

To France nor Flanders dare we pass,
  Nor Bourdeaux voyage dare we fare; *
And all for a rover that lies on the seas,
  Who robs us of our merchant ware.

King Henry frowned, and turned him round,
  And swore by the Lord, that was mickle of might,
I thought he had not been in the world,
  Durst have wrought England such unright.
The merchants sighed, and said, alas!
  And thus they did their answer frame,
He is a proud Scot, that robs on the seas,
  And Sir Andrew Barton is his name.

The king looked over his left shoulder,
  And an angry look then looked he:
Have I never a lord in all my realm,
  Will fetch yon traitor unto me?
Yea, that dare I, lord Howard says;
  Yea, that dare I with heart and hand;
If it please your grace to give me leave,
  Myself will be the only man.

* Travel.

Thou art but young, the king replied;
　Yon Scot hath numbered many a year.
Trust me, my liege, I'll make him quail,
　Or before my prince I will never appear.
Then bowmen and gunners thou shalt have,
　And choose them over my realm so free;
Besides good mariners, and ship-boys,
　To guide the great ship on the sea.

The first man that lord Howard chose
　Was the ablest gunner in all the realm,
Though he was threescore years and ten;
　Good Peter Simon was his name.
Peter, says he, I must to the sea,
　To bring home a traitor live or dead;
Before all others I have chosen thee,
　Of a hundred gunners to be the head.

If you, my lord, have chosen me
　Of a hundred gunners to be the head,
Then hang me up on your main-mast tree,
　If I miss my mark one shilling bread.*

　　　　* Breadth.

My lord then chose a bowman rare,
  Whose active hands had gained fame ;
In Yorkshire was this gentleman born,
  And William Horseley was his name.

Horseley, said he, I must with speed
  Go seek a traitor on the sea,
And now of a hundred bowmen brave
  To be the head I have chosen thee.
If you, quoth he, have chosen me
  Of a hundred bowmen to be the head,
On your main-màst I'll hanged be,
  If I miss, twelvescore,* one penny bread.

With pikes and guns, and bowmen bold,
  This noble Howard is gone to the sea ;
With a valiant heart and a pleasant cheer,
  Out at Thames mouth sailed he.
And days he scant had sailed three
  Upon the voyage he took in hand,
But there he met with a noble ship,
  And stoutly made it stay and stand.

* Twelvescore paces off.

Thou must tell me, lord Howard said,
  Now who thou art and what's thy name,
And show me where thy dwelling is,
  And whither bound, and whence thou came.
My name is Henry Hunt, quoth he
  With a heavy heart, and a careful mind ;
I and my ship do both belong
  To the Newcastle that stands upon Tyne.

Hast thou not heard, now, Henry Hunt,
  As thou hast sailed by day and by night,
Of a Scottish rover on the seas ;
  Men call him sir Andrew Barton, knight ?
Then ever he sighed, and said alas !
  With a grieved mind, and well away !
But over-well I know that wight,
  I was his prisoner yesterday.

As I was sailing upon the sea,
  A Bourdeaux voyage for to fare ;
To his hatchboard * he clasped me,
  And robbed me of all my merchant ware :

* Part of the side of the ship.

Sir Andrew Barton.

And mickle debts, God wot, I owe,
  And every man will have his own,
And I am now to London bound,
  Of our gracious king to beg a boon.

That shall not need, lord Howard says;
  Let me but once that robber see,
For every penny ta'en thee fro'
  It shall be doubled shillings three.
Now God forefend, the merchant said,
  That you should seek so far amiss!
God keep you out of that traitor's hands!
  Full little ye wot what a man he is.

He is brass within, and steel without,
  With beams on his topcastle strong;
And eighteen pieces of ordinance
  He carries on each side along:
And he hath a pinnace dearly dight,*
  St. Andrew's cross that is his guide;
His pinnace beareth ninescore men,
  And fifteen cannons on each side.

* Fitted out.

I

Were ye twenty ships, and he but one,
   I swear by kirk, and bower, and hall,
He would overcome them every one,
   If once his beams they do down fall.
This is cold comfort, says my lord,
   To welcome a stranger thus to the sea :
Yet I'll bring him and his ship to shore,
   Or to Scotland he shall carry me.

Then a noble gunner you must have,
   And he must aim well with his ee,
And sink his pinnace into the sea,
   Or else he ne'er o'ercome will be :
And if you chance his ship to board,
   This counsel I must give withal,
Let no man to his topcastle go
   To strive to let his beams down fall.

And seven pieces of ordinance,
   I pray your honour lend to me,
On each side of my ship along,
   And I will lead you on the sea.

A glass I'll set, that may be seen,
   Whether you sail by day or night ;
And to-morrow, I swear, by nine of the clock
   You shall meet with Sir Andrew Barton, knight.

SIR ANDREW BARTON.

THE SECOND PART.

THE merchant set my lord a glass
    So well apparent in his sight,
And on the morrow, by nine of the clock,
    He showed him Sir Andrew Barton, knight.
His hatchbord it was gilt with gold,
    So dearly dight it dazzled the ee :
Now by my faith, lord Howard says,
    This is a gallant sight to see.

Take in your ancients,* standards eke,
    So close that no man may them see ;
And put me forth a white willow wand,
    As merchants use to sail the sea.

* Flags.

But they stirred neither top, nor mast;*
Stoutly they passed Sir Andrew by.
What English churls are yonder, he said,
That can so little courtesy?

Now by the rood, three years and more,
I have been admiral over the sea;
And never an English nor Portingall †
Without my leave can pass this way.
Then called he forth his stout pinnàce;
Fetch back yon pedlars now to me:
I swear by the mass, yon English churls
Shall all hang at my main-mast tree.

With that the pinnace it shot off,
Full well lord Howard might it ken;
For it stroke down my lord's fore mast,
And killed fourteen of his men.
Come hither, Simon, says my lord,
Look that thy word be true, thou said;
For at my main-mast thou shalt hang,
If thou miss thy mark one shilling bread.

---

* *i.e.* Did not salute.   † Portuguese.

Simon was old, but his heart it was bold,
   His ordinance he laid right low;
He put in chain full nine yards long,
   With other great shot less, and moe;
And he let go his great gun's shot:
   So well he settled it with his ee,
The first sight that Sir Andrew saw,
   He saw his pinnace sunk in the sea.

And when he saw his pinnace sunk,
   Lord, how his heart with rage did swell!
Now cut my ropes, it is time to be gone;
   I'll fetch yon pedlars back mysel'.
When my lord saw Sir Andrew loose,
   Within his heart he was full fain:
Now spread your ancients, strike up drums,
   Sound all your trumpets out amain.

Fight on, my men, Sir Andrew says,
   Well howsoever this gear will sway;*
It is my lord admiral of Englànd,
   Is come to seek me on the sea.

      * However this affair will end.

Simon had a son, who shot right well,
  That did Sir Andrew mickle scare;
In at his deck he gave a shot,
  Killed threescore of his men of war.

Then Henry Hunt with rigour hot
  Came bravely on the other side,
Soon he drove down his fore-mast tree,
  And killed fourscore men beside.
Now, out alas! Sir Andrew cried,
  What may a man now think, or say?
Yonder merchant thief, that pierceth me,
  He was my prisoner yesterday.

Come hither to me, thou Gordon good,
  That aye wast ready at my call;
I will give thee three hundred marks,
  If thou wilt let my beams down fall.
Lord Howard he then call'd in haste,
  Horseley see thou be true instead;
For thou shalt at the main-mast hang,
  If thou miss, twelvescore, one penny bread.

Then Gordon swarved * the main-mast tree,
  He swarved it with might and main ;
But Horseley with a bearing arrow,
  Stroke the Gordon through the brain ;
And he fell into the hatches again,
  And sore his deadly wound did bleed :
Then word went through Sir Andrew's men,
  How that the Gordon he was dead.

Come hither to me, James Hambilton,
  Thou art my only sister's son,
If thou wilt let my beams down fall,
  Six hundred nobles thou hast won.
With that he swarved the main-mast tree,
  He swarved it with nimble art ;
But Horseley with a broad arrow
  Pierced the Hambilton through the heart :

And down he fell upon the deck,
  That with his blood did stream amain :
Then every Scot cried, Well-away !
  Alas, a comely youth is slain !

* Climbed.

Sir Andrew Barton.

All woe begone was Sir Andrew then,
  With grief and rage his heart did swell:
Go fetch me forth my armour of proof,
  For I will to the topcastle mysel'.

Go fetch me forth my armour of proof;
  That gilded is with gold so clear:
God be with my brother John of Barton!
  Against the Portingalls he it ware:
And when he had on this armour of proof,
  He was a gallant sight to see:
Ah! ne'er didst thou meet with living wight,
  My dear brother, could cope with thee.

Come hither Horseley, says my lord,
  And look your shaft that it go right,
Shoot a good shot in time of need,
  And for it thou shalt be made a knight.
I'll shoot my best, quoth Horseley then,
  Your honour shall see, with might and main;
But if I was hanged at your main-mast,
  I have now left but arrows twain.

Sir Andrew he did swarve the tree,
　With right good will he swarved then:
Upon his breast did Horseley hit,
　But the arrow bounded back again.
Then Horseley spied a privy place
　With a perfect eye in a secret part;
Under the spole * of his right arm
　He smote Sir Andrew to the heart.

Fight on, my men, Sir Andrew says,
　A little I'm hurt, but yet not slain;
I'll but lie down and bleed awhile,
　And then I'll rise and fight again.
Fight on, my men, Sir Andrew says,
　And never flinch before the foe;
And stand fast by St. Andrew's cross
　Until you hear my whistle blow.

They never heard his whistle blow,——
　Which made their hearts wax sore adread:
Then Horseley said, Aboard, my lord,
　For well I wot, Sir Andrew's dead.

* The arm-pit.

SIR ANDREW BARTON

They boarded then his noble ship,
  They boarded it with might and main ;
Eighteen score Scots alive they found,
  The rest were either maimed or slain.

Lord Howard took a sword in hand,
  And off he smote Sir Andrew's head,
I must have left England many a day,
  If thou wert alive as thou art dead.
He caused his body to be cast
  Over the hatchboard into the sea,
And about his middle three hundred crowns :
  Wherever thou land this will bury thee.

Thus from the wars lord Howard came,
  And back he sailèd o'er the main,
With mickle joy and triumphìng
  Into Thames mouth he came again.
Lord Howard then a letter wrote,
  And sealèd it with seal and ring ;
Such a noble prize have I brought to your grace,
  As never did subject to a king :

Sir Andrew's ship I bring with me ;
  A braver ship was never none :
Now hath your grace two ships of war,
  Before in England was but one.
King Henry's grace with royal cheer
  Welcomed the noble Howard home,
And where, said he, is this rover stout,
  That I myself may give the doom ?

The rover, he is safe, my liege,
  Full many a fathom in the sea ;
If he were alive as he is dead,
  I must have left England many a day :
And your grace may thank four men i' the ship
  For the victory which we have won,
These are William Horseley, Henry Hunt,
  And Peter Simon, and his son.

To Henry Hunt, the king then said,
  In lieu of what was from thee ta'en,
A noble a-day now thou shalt have,
  Sir Andrew's jewels and his chain.

And Horseley thou shalt be a knight,
  And lands and livings shalt have store ;
Howard shall be earl of Surrey hight,
  As Howards erst have been before.

Now, Peter Simon, thou art old,
  I will maintain thee and thy son :
And the men shall have five hundred marks
  For the good service they have done.
Then in came the queen with ladies fair
  To see Sir Andrew Barton knight :
They ween'd that he were brought on shore,
  And thought to have seen a gallant sight.

But when they saw his deadly face,
  And eyes so hollow in his head,
I would give, quoth the king, a thousand marks,
  This man were alive as he is dead :
Yet for the manful part he played,
  Which fought so well with heart and hand,
His men shall have twelvepence a day,
  Till they come to my brother king's high land.

BRAVE LORD WILLOUGHBEY.*

THE fifteenth day of July,
 With glistering spear and shield,
A famous fight in Flanders
 Was foughten on the field:
The most courageous officers
 Were English captains three;
But the bravest man in battle
 Was brave lord Willoughbèy.

The next was captain Norris,
 A valiant man was he:
The other captain Turner,
 From field would never flee.

* Peregrine Bertie, Lord Willoughbey of Eresby, died 1601.

With fifteen hundred fighting men,
  Alas ! there were no more,
They fought with fourteen thousand then,
  Upon the bloody shore.

Stand to it noble pikemen,
  And look you round about :
And shoot you right you bowmen,
  And we will keep them out :
You musket and calliver* men,
  Do you prove true to me,
I'll be the foremost man in fight,
  Says brave lord Willoughbèy.

And then the bloody enemy
  They fiercely did assail,
And fought it out most furiously,
  Not doubting to prevail :
The wounded men on both sides fell
  Most piteous for to see,
Yet nothing could the courage quell
  Of brave lord Willoughbèy.

  * A kind of gun.

For seven hours to all men's view
  This fight endured sore,
Until our men so feeble grew,
  That they could fight no more;
And then upon dead horses
  Full savourly they ate,
And drank the puddle water,
  They could no better get.

When they had fed so freely,
  They kneeled on the ground,
And praised God devoutly
  For the favour they had found;
And beating up their colours,
  The fight they did renew,
And turning tow'rds the Spaniard,
  A thousand more they slew.

The sharp steel-pointed arrows,
  And bullets thick did fly;
Then did our valiant soldiers
  Charge on most furiously;

Page 179

THE BRAVE LORD WILLOUGHBEY

Which made the Spaniards waver,
  They thought it best to flee,
They fear'd the stout behaviour
  Of brave lord Willoughbèy.

Then quoth the Spanish general,
  Come let us march away,
I fear we shall be spoiled all,
  If here we longer stay;
For yonder comes lord Willoughbey
  With courage fierce and fell,
He will not give one inch of way
  For all the devils in hell.

And then the fearful enemy
  Was quickly put to flight,
Our men pursued courageously,
  And caught their forces quite;
But at last they gave a shout,
  Which echoed through the sky,
God, and St. George for England!
  The conquerors did cry.

K

This news was brought to England
  With all the speed might be,
And soon our gracious queen was told
  Of this same victory.
O this is brave lord Willoughbey,
  My love that ever won,
Of all the lords of honour,
  'Tis he great deeds hath done.

To the soldiers that were maimed,
  And wounded in the fray,
The queen allowed a pension
  Of fifteen pence a day;
And from all costs and charges
  She quit and set them free:
And this she did all for the sake
  Of brave lord Willoughbèy.

Then courage, noble Englishmen,
  And never be dismayed:
If that we be but one to ten,
  We will not be afraid

To fight with foreign enemies,
  And set our nation free.
And thus I end the bloody bout
  Of brave lord Willoughbèy.

KING JOHN AND THE ABBOT OF CANTERBURY.

AN ancient story I'll tell you anon
    Of a notable prince, that was called king John ;
    And he ruled England with main and with
        might,
    For he did great wrong, and maintain'd little
        right.

And I'll tell you a story, a story so merry,
Concerning the Abbot of Canterbury ;
How for his house-keeping, and high renown,
They rode post for him to fair London town.

An hundred men, the king did hear say,
The abbot kept in his house every day ;
And fifty gold chains, without any doubt,
In velvet coats waited the abbot about.

How now, father abbot, I hear it of thee,
Thou keepest a far better house than me,
And for thy house-keeping and high renown,
I fear thou work'st treason against my crown.

My liege, quoth the abbot, I would it were known,
I never spend nothing, but what is my own;
And I trust, your grace will do me no deer,*
For spending of my own true-gotten gear.

Yes, yes, father abbot, thy fault it is high,
And now for the same thou needest must die;
For except thou canst answer me questions three,
Thy head shall be smitten from thy body.

And first, quoth the king, when I'm in this stead,†
With my crown of gold so fair on my head,
Among all my liege-men so noble of birth,
Thou must tell me to one penny what I am worth.

Secondly, tell me, without any doubt,
How soon I may ride the whole world about.
And at the third question thou must not shrink,
But tell me here truly what I do think.

* Hurt. † Place.

O, these are hard questions for my shallow wit,
Nor I cannot answer your grace as yet:
But if you will give me but three weeks' space,
I'll do my endeavour to answer your grace.

Now three weeks' space to thee will I give,
And that is the longest time thou hast to live;
For if thou dost not answer my questions three,
Thy lands and thy livings are forfeit to me.

Away rode the abbot all sad at that word,
And he rode to Cambridge, and Oxenford;
But never a doctor there was so wise,
That could with his learning an answer devise.

Then home rode the abbot of comfort so cold,
And he met his shepherd a going to fold:
How now, my lord abbot, you are welcome home;
What news do you bring us from good king John?

Sad news, sad news, shepherd, I must give;
That I have but three days more to live:
For if I do not answer him questions three,
My head will be smitten from my bod'.

THE ABBOT OF CANTERBURY

The first is to tell him there in that stead,
With his crown of gold so fair on his head,
Among all his liege-men so noble of birth,
To within one penny of what he is worth.

The second, to tell him, without any doubt,
How soon he may ride this whole world about :
And at the third question I must not shrink,
But tell him there truly what he does think.

Now cheer up, sire abbot, did you never hear yet,
That a fool he may learn a wise man wit ?
Lend me horse, and serving men, and your apparel,
And I'll ride to London to answer your quarrel.

Nay frown not, if it hath been told unto me,
I am like your lordship, as ever may be :
And if you will but lend me your gown,
There is none shall know us at fair London town.

Now horses, and serving-men thou shalt have,
With sumptuous array most gallant and brave ;
With crozier, and mitre, and rochet, and cope,
Fit to appear 'fore our father the pope.

Now welcome, sire abbot, the king he did say,
'Tis well thou'rt come back to keep thy day ;
For and if thou canst answer my questions three,
Thy life and thy living both saved shall be.

And first, when thou seest me here in this stead,
With my crown of gold so fair on my head,
Among all my liege-men so noble of birth,
Tell me to one penny what I am worth.

For thirty pence our Saviour was sold
Among the false Jews, as I have been told ;
And twenty-nine is the worth of thee,
For I think, thou art one penny worser than he.

The king he laughed, and swore by St. Bittel,*
I did not think I had been worth so little !
—Now secondly tell me, without any doubt,
How soon I may ride this whole world about.

You must rise with the sun, and ride with the same,
Until the next morning he riseth again ;
And then your grace need not make any doubt,
But in twenty-four hours you'll ride it about.

* St. Botolph.

The king he laughed, and swore by St. Jone,
I did not think it could be gone so soon!
—Now from the third question thou must not shrink,
But tell me here truly what I do think.

Yea, that shall I do, and make your grace merry :
You think I'm the abbot of Canterbùry ;
But I'm his poor shepherd, as plain you may see,
That am come to beg pardon for him and for me.

The king he laughed, and swore by the mass,
I'll make thee lord abbot this day in his place !
Now nay, my liege, be not in such speed,
For, alack, I can neither write nor read.

Four nobles a week then I will give thee,
For this merry jest thou hast shown unto me ;
And tell the old abbot when thou com'st home,
Thou hast brought him a pardon from good king John.

ROBIN HOOD AND THE CURTAL FRIAR.

IN the summer time, when leaves grow green,
    And flowers are fresh and gay,
Robin Hood and his merry men
    Were all disposed to play.

Then some would leap, and some would run,
    And some would use artillery;
Which of you can a good bow draw,
    A good archer for to be?

Which of you can kill a buck?
    Or who can kill a doe?
Or who can kill a hart of grease,*
    Five hundred foot him fro'?

* Fat hart.

Will Scarlet he kill'd a buck,
  And Midge he kill'd a doe;
And Little John kill'd a hart of grease,
  Five hundred foot him fro'.

God's blessing on thy heart, said Robin Hood,
  That shot such a shot for me;
I would ride my horse an hundred miles
  To find one to match thee.

That caused Will Scarlet to laugh,
  He laugh'd full heartily;
There lives a friar in Fountain's Abbey
  Will beat both him and thee.

The curtal friar in Fountain's Abbey
  Well can draw a good strong bow;
He will beat both you and your yeomen,
  Set them all on a row.

Robin Hood took a solemn oath,
  It was by Mary free,
That he would neither eat nor drink,
  Till the friar he did see.

Robin Hood put on his harness good,
  On his head a cap of steel ;
Broad sword and buckler by his side,
  And they became him well.

He took his bow into his hand,
  (It was of a trusty tree)
With a sheaf of arrows by his side
  And to Fountain Dale went he.

And coming unto fair Fountain Dale,
  No farther would he ride :
There was he 'ware of a curtal friar,
  Walking by the water-side.

The friar had on a harness good,
  On his head a cap of steel ;
Broad sword and buckler by his side,
  And they became him well.

Robin Hood lighted off his horse,
  And tied him to a thorn :
Carry me over the water, thou curtal friar,
  Or else thy life's forlorn.

ROBIN HOOD AND THE CURTAL FRIAR

The friar took Robin Hood on his back,
  Deep water he did bestride,
And spake neither good word nor bad
  Till he came to the other side.

Lightly leap'd Robin off the friar's back,
  The friar said to him again,
Carry me over the water, fine fellow,
  Or it shall breed thee pain.

Robin Hood took the friar on his back,
  Deep water he did bestride,
And spake neither good nor bad
  Till he came to the other side.

Lightly leap'd the friar off Robin Hood's back,
  Robin said to him again,
Carry me over the water thou curtal friar,
  Or it shall breed thee pain.

The friar he took Robin Hood on his back again
  And stepp'd up to his knee ;
Till he came to the middle of the stream
  Neither good nor bad spake he ;

And coming to the middle of the stream
  There he threw Robin in ;
And choose thee, choose thee, fine fellow,
  Whether thou wilt sink or swim.

Robin Hood swam to a bush of broom,
  The friar to the willow wand ;
Bold Robin Hood he got to the shore,
  And took his bow in his hand.

One of the best arrows under his belt
  To the friar he let fly :
The curtal friar with his steel buckler
  Did put that arrow by.

Shoot on, shoot on, thou fine fellow,
  Shoot as thou hast begun ;
If thou shoot here a summer's day,
  Thy mark I will not shun.

Robin Hood shot so passing well,
  Till his arrows all were gone ;
They took their swords and steel bucklers,
  They fought with might and main.

From ten o'clock that very day,
   Till four i' the afternoon;
Then Robin Hood came on his knees,
   Of the friar to beg a boon.

A boon, a boon, thou curtal friar,
   I beg it on my knee;
Give me leave to set my horn to my mouth,
   And to blow blasts three.

That I will do, said the curtal friar,
   Of thy blasts I have no doubt;
I hope thou wilt blow so passing well,
   Till both thy eyes drop out.

Robin Hood set his horn to his mouth,
   And he blew out blasts three,
Half a hundred yeomen, with their bows bent,
   Came ranging over the lea.

Whose men are these, said the friar,
   That come so hastily?
These men are mine, said Robin Hood,
   Friar, what's that to thee?

A boon, a boon, said the curtal friar,
  The like I gave to thee;
Give me leave to put my fist to my mouth,
  And whute * whutes three.

That I will do, said Robin Hood,
  Or else I were to blame;
Three whutes in a friar's fist
  Would make me glad and fain.

The friar he set his fist to his mouth,
  And he whuted him whutes three;
Half an hundred good ban dogs
  Came running over the lea.

Here is for every man a dog,
  And I myself for thee;
Nay, by my faith, said Robin Hood,
  Friar, that may not be.

Two dogs at once to Robin did go,
  The one behind, and the other before;
Robin Hood's mantle of Lincoln green
  Off from his back they tore.

* Whistle.

And whether his men shot east or west,
  Or they shot north or south,
The curtal dogs, so taught they were,
  They caught the arrows in their mouth.

Take up thy dogs, said Little John,
  Friar, at my bidding thee;
Whose man art thou, said the curtal friar,
  That comes here to prate to me?

I am Little John, Robin Hood's man,
  Friar, I will not lie;
If thou take not up thy dogs anon,
  I'll take them up and thee.

Little John had a bow in his hand,
  He shot with might and main;
Soon half a score of the friar's dogs
  Lay dead upon the plain.

Hold thy hand, good fellow, said the curtal friar,
  Thy master and I will agree;
And we will have new orders taken,
  With all haste that may be.

L

If thou wilt forsake fair Fountain Dale,
  And Fountain Abbey free,
Every Sunday throughout the year
  A noble shall be thy fee.

Every Sunday throughout the year,
  Chang'd shall thy garments be,
If thou wilt to fair Nottingham go,
  And there remain with me.

The curtal friar had kept Fountain Dale,
  Seven long years and more;
There was neither knight, lord, nor earl,
  Could make him yield before.

ROBIN HOOD AND ALLEN-À-DALE.

OME listen to me, you gallants so free,
   All you that love mirth for to hear,
And I will tell you of a bold outlaw,
   That liv'd in Nottinghamshire.

As Robin Hood in the forest stood,
   All under the greenwood tree,
There was he aware of a brave young man,
   As fine as fine might be.

The youngster was clothed in scarlet red,
   In scarlet fine and gay;
And he did frisk it o'er the plain,
   And chaunted a roundelay.

As Robin Hood next morning stood
  Amongst the leaves so gay,
There did he 'spy the same young man
  Come drooping along the way.

The scarlet he wore the day before,
  It was cast clean away ;
And ev'ry step he fetch'd a sigh,
  Alack and well a day !

Then stepped forth brave Little John,
  And Midge the miller's son,
Which made the young man bend his bow,
  When he did see them come.

Stand off, stand off, the young man said,
  What is your will with me ?
You must come before our master straight,
  Under yonder greenwood tree.

And when he came bold Robin before,
  Robin asked him courteously,
O hast thou any money to spare
  For my merry men and me ?

I have no money, the young man said,
   But five shillings and a ring,
And that I have kept these seven long years,
   To have it at my wedding.

Yesterday I should have married a maid,
   But from me she was ta'en,
And chosen to be an old knight's delight,
   Whereby my poor heart is slain.

What is thy name then, said Robin Hood,
   Come, tell me without fail?
By the faith of my body, then said the young man,
   My name is Allen-a-Dale.

What wilt thou give me, said Robin Hood,
   In ready gold or fee,
To help thee to thy true love again,
   And deliver her unto thee?

I have no money, then quoth the young man,
   No ready gold or fee,
But I will swear upon a book,
   Thy true servant for to be.

How many miles is it to thy true love?
    Come, tell me without any guile.
By the faith of my body, then said the young man,
    It is but five little mile.

Then Robin he hasted over the plain,
    And he did neither stint nor lin,*
Until he came unto the church,
    Where Allen should have kept his wedding!

What dost thou here, the Bishop then said,
    I prithee tell unto me?
I am a bold harper, quoth Robin Hood,
    And the best in the north country.

O welcome, O welcome, the bishop then said,
    That music best pleaseth me;
You shall have no music, quoth Robin Hood,
    Till the bride and bridegroom I see.

With that came in a wealthy knight,
    Who was both grave and old;
And after him a finikin lass,
    That did shine like glittering gold.

            * Stop.

THE MARRIAGE OF ALLEN A DALE

This is not a fit match, quoth bold Robin Hood,
    That you do seem to make here;
For since we are come into the church,
    The bride shall choose her own dear.

Then Robin Hood put his horn to his mouth,
    And blew blasts two or three;
Then four and twenty bowmen bold
    Came leaping over the lea.

And when they came into the churchyard,
    Marching all on a row,
The first man was Allen-a-Dale,
    To give bold Robin his bow.

This is thy true love, Robin he said,
    Young Allen, as I have heard say,
And thou shalt be married at this same time,
    Before we depart away.

That shalt not be, the bishop he said,
    For thy word shall not stand;
They shall be three times asked in the church,
    As the law is of our land.

Robin Hood pull'd off the bishop's coat,
   And put it upon Little John;
By the faith of my body, then Robin he said,
   This cloth doth make thee a man.

When Little John went to the quire,
   The people began to laugh:
He ask'd them seven times in the church,
   Lest three times should not be enough.

Who gives this maid? said Little John;
   Quoth Robin, that do I;
And he that takes her from Allen-a-Dale,
   Full dearly shall her buy.

And thus having ended this merry wedding,
   The bride she looked like a queen!
And so they returned to the merry green wood,
   Amongst the leaves so green.

VALENTINE AND URSINE.

HEN Flora 'gins to deck the fields
   With colours fresh and fine,
Then holy clerks their matins sing
   To good Saint Valentine!

The king of France that morning fair
   He would a hunting ride:
To Artois forest prancing forth
   In all his princely pride.

To grace his sports a courtly train
   Of gallant peers attend;
And with their loud and cheerful cries
   The hills and valleys rend.

Through the deep forest swift they pass,
  Through woods and thickets wild ;
When down within a lonely dell
  They found a new-born child ;

All in a scarlet kercher laid
  Of silk so fine and thin :
A golden mantle wrapt him round
  Pinn'd with a silver pin.

The sudden sight surpris'd them all ;
  The courtiers gather'd round ;
They look, they call, the mother seek ;
  No mother could be found.

At length the king himself drew near,
  And as he gazing stands,
The pretty babe look'd up and smil'd,
  And stretch'd his little hands.

Now, by the rood, king Pepin says,
  This child is passing fair :
I wot he is of gentle blood ;
  Perhaps some prince's heir.

Go bear him home unto my court
   With all the care ye may:
Let him be christen'd Valentine,
   In honour of this day:

And look me out some cunning nurse;
   Well nurtur'd let him be:
Nor aught be wanting that becomes
   A bairn of high degree.

They look'd him out a cunning nurse,
   And nurtur'd well was he;
Nor aught was wanting that became
   A bairn of high degree.

Thus grew the little Valentine,
   Belov'd of king and peers;
And show'd in all he spake or did
   A wit beyond his years.

But chief in gallant feats of arms
   He did himself advance,
And ere he grew to man's estate
   He had no peer in France.

And now the early down began
  To shade his youthful chin;
When Valentine was dubb'd a knight,
  That he might glory win.

A boon, a boon, my gracious liege,
  I beg a boon of thee!
The first adventure that befalls
  May be reserv'd for me.

The first adventure shall be thine,
  The king did smiling say.
Nor many days, when lo! there came
  Three palmers clad in gray.

Help, gracious lord, they weeping said;
  And knelt, as it was meet:
From Artois forest we be come,
  With weak and weary feet.

Within those deep and dreary woods
  There wends a savage boy;
Whose fierce and mortal rage doth yield
  Thy subjects dire annoy.

'Mong ruthless bears he sure was bred ;
   He lurks within their den :
With bears he lives, with bears he feeds,
   And drinks the blood of men.

To more than savage strength he joins
   A more than human skill :
For arms, no cunning may suffice
   His cruel rage to still :

Up then rose sir Valentine,
   And claim'd that arduous deed.
Go forth and conquer, said the king,
   And great shall be thy meed.

Well mounted on a milk-white steed,
   His armour white as snow ;
As well beseem'd a virgin knight,
   Who ne'er had fought a foe :

To Artois forest he repairs
   With all the haste he may ;
And soon he spies the savage youth
   A rending of his prey.

His unkempt hair all matted hung
　His shaggy shoulders round :
His eager eye all fiery glow'd :
　His face with fury frown'd.

Like eagle's talons grew his nails :
　His limbs were thick and strong;
And dreadful was the knotted oak
　He bare with him along.

Soon as sir Valentine approach'd,
　He starts with sudden spring ;
And yelling forth a hideous howl,
　He made the forests ring.

As when a tiger fierce and fell
　Hath spied a passing roe,
And leaps at once upon his throat ;
　So sprung the savage foe.

So lightly leap'd with furious force
　The gentle knight to seize :
But met his tall uplifted spear,
　Which sunk him on his knees.

A second stroke so stiff and stern
   Had laid the savage low;
But springing up, he rais'd his club,
   And aim'd a dreadful blow.

The watchful warrior bent his head,
   And shunn'd the coming stroke;
Upon his taper spear it fell,
   And all to shivers broke.

Then lighting nimbly from his steed,
   He drew his burnished brand:
The savage quick as lightning flew
   To wrest it from his hand.

Three times he grasp'd the silver hilt;
   Three times he felt the blade;
Three times it fell with furious force;
   Three ghastly wounds it made.

Now with redoubled rage he roar'd;
   His eye-ball flash'd with fire;
Each hairy limb with fury shook;
   And all his heart was ire.

Then closing fast with furious gripe
    He clasp'd the champion round,
And with a strong and sudden twist
    He laid him on the ground.

But soon the knight, with active spring,
    O'erturn'd his hairy foe :
And now between their sturdy fists
    Passed many a bruising blow.

They roll'd and grappled on the ground,
    And there they struggled long :
Skilful and active was the knight ;
    The savage he was strong.

But brutal force and savage strength
    To art and skill must yield :
Sir Valentine at length prevail'd,
    And won the well-fought field.

Then binding straight his conquer'd foe
    Fast with an iron chain,
He ties him to his horse's tail,
    And leads him o'er the plain.

Page 161

VALENTINE AND URSINE

.

.

To court his hairy captive soon
   Sir Valentine doth bring;
And kneeling down upon his knee,
   Presents him to the king.

With loss of blood and loss of strength,
   The savage tamer grew;
And to sir Valentine became
   A servant tried and true.

And 'cause with bears he erst was bred,
   Ursine they call his name;
A name which unto future times
   The Muses shall proclaim.

In high renown with prince and peer
    Now liv'd sir Valentine :
His high renown with prince and peer
    Made envious hearts repine.

It chanc'd the king upon a day
    Prepar'd a sumptuous feast :
And there came lords and dainty dames,
    And many a noble guest.

Amid their cups, that freely flow'd,
    Their revelry, and mirth,
A youthful knight tax'd Valentine
    Of base and doubtful birth.

The foul reproach, so grossly urg'd,
　His generous heart did wound :
And straight he vow'd he ne'er would rest
　Till he his parents found.

Then bidding king and peers adieu,
　Early one summer's day,
With faithful Ursine by his side,
　From court he took his way.

O'er hill and valley, moss and moor,
　For many a day they pass ;
At length, upon a moated lake,*
　They found a bridge of brass.

Beyond it rose a castle fair,
　Y-built of marble stone :
The battlements were gilt with gold,
　And glittered in the sun.

Beneath the bridge, with strange device,
　A hundred bells were hung ;
That man, nor beast, might pass thereon,
　But straight their larum rung.

* *i. c.* a lake that served for a moat to a castle.

This quickly found the youthful pair,
    Who boldly crossing o'er,
The jangling sound bedeaft their ears,
    And rung from shore to shore.

Quick at the sound the castle gates
    Unlock'd and opened wide,
And straight a giant huge and grim
    Stalk'd forth with stately pride.

Now yield you, caitiffs, to my will,
    He cried with hideous roar;
Or else the wolves shall eat your flesh,
    And ravens drink your gore.

Vain boaster, said the youthful knight,
    I scorn thy threats and thee:
I trust to force thy brazen gates,
    And set thy captives free.

Then putting spurs unto his steed,
    He aim'd a dreadful thrust;
The spear against the giant glanc'd,
    And caus'd the blood to burst.

Mad and outrageous with the pain,
    He whirl'd his mace of steel :
The very wind of such a blow
    Had made the champion reel.

It haply missed ; and now the knight
    His glittering sword display'd,
And riding round with whirlwind speed
    Oft made him feel the blade.

As when a large and monstrous oak
    Unceasing axes hew :
So fast around the giant's limbs
    The blows quick-darting flew.

As when the boughs with hideous fall
    Some hapless woodman crush :
With such a force the enormous foe
    Did on the champion rush.

A fearful blow, alas ! there came,
    Both horse and knight it took,
And laid them senseless in the dust ;
    So fatal was the stroke.

Then smiling forth a hideous grin,
   The giant strides in haste,
And, stooping, aims a second stroke :
   Now, caitiff, breathe thy last !

But ere it fell, two thundering blows
   Upon his scull descend :
From Ursine's knotty club they came,
   Who ran to save his friend.

Down sank the giant gaping wide,
   And rolling his grim eyes :
The hairy youth repeats his blows :
   He gasps, he groans, he dies.

Quickly sir Valentine reviv'd,
   With Ursine's timely care :
And now to search the castle walls
   The venturous youths repair.

The blood and bones of murder'd knight
   They found where'er they came :
At length within a lonely cell
   They saw a mournful dame.

Her gentle eyes were dimm'd with tears;
   Her cheeks were pale with woe;
And long sir Valentine besought
   Her doleful tale to know.

Alas! young knight, she weeping said,
   Condole my wretched fate;
A childless mother here you see;
   A wife without a mate.

These twenty winters here forlorn
   I've drawn my hated breath;
Sole witness of a monster's crimes,
   And wishing aye for death.

Know, I am sister of a king,
   And in my early years
Was married to a mighty prince,
   The fairest of his peers.

With him I sweetly liv'd in love
   A twelvemonth and a day:
When, lo! a foul and treacherous priest
   Y-wrought our loves' decay.

His seeming goodness won him pow'r;
  He had his master's ear :
And long to me and all the world
  He did a saint appear.

One day, when we were all alone,
  He proffer'd odious love :
The wretch with horror I repuls'd,
  And from my presence drove.

He feign'd remorse, and piteous begg'd
  His crime I'd not reveal :
Which, for his seeming penitence,
  I promis'd to conceal.

With treason, villainy, and wrong,
  My goodness he repay'd :
With jealous doubts he fill'd my lord,
  And me to woe betray'd.

He hid a slave within my bed,
  Then rais'd a bitter cry.
My lord, possess'd with rage, condemn'd
  Me, all unheard, to die.

But 'cause I then was great with child,
   At length my life he spar'd :
But bade me instant quit the realm,
   One trusty knight my guard.

Forth on my journey I depart,
   Oppressed with grief and woe :
And tow'rds my brother's distant court,
   With breaking heart, I go.

Long time thro' sundry foreign lands
   We slowly pace along :
At length, within a forest wild,
   I fell in labour strong :

And while the knight for succour sought,
   And left me there forlorn,
My childbed pains so fast increas'd
   Two lovely boys were born.

The eldest fair and smooth as snow
   That tips the mountain hoar ;
The younger's little body rough
   With hairs was cover'd o'er.

But here afresh begin my woes:
  While tender care I took
To shield my eldest from the cold,
  And wrap him in my cloak,

A prowling bear burst from the wood,
  And seiz'd my younger son:
Affection lent my weakness wings,
  And after them I run.

But all forwearied, weak, and spent,
  I quickly swoon'd away;
And there beneath the greenwood shade
  Long time I lifeless lay.

At length the knight brought me relief,
  And rais'd me from the ground:
But neither of my pretty babes
  Could ever more be found.

And, while in search we wander'd far,
  We met that giant grim;
Who ruthless slew my trusty knight,
  And bare me off with him.

But charm'd by heav'n, or else my griefs,
 He offer'd me no wrong ;
Save that within these lonely walls
 I've been immur'd so long.

Now surely, said the youthful knight,
 You are lady Ballisance,
Wife to the Grecian Emperor :
 Your brother's king of France.

For in your royal 'brother's court
 Myself my breeding had ;
Where oft the story of your woes
 Hath made my bosom sad.

If so, know your accuser's dead,
 And dying own'd his crime ;
And long your lord hath sought you out
 Thro' every foreign clime.

And when no tidings he could learn
 Of his much wrongèd wife,
He vow'd thenceforth within his court
 To lead a hermit's life.

Now heaven is kind! the lady said;
   And dropped a joyful tear:
Shall I once more behold my lord?
   That lord I love so dear?

But, madam, said sir Valentine,
   And knelt upon his knee;
Know you the cloak that wrapt your babe,
   If you the same should see?

And pulling forth the cloth of gold,
   In which himself was found;
The lady gave a sudden shriek,
   And fainted on the ground.

But by his pious care reviv'd,
   His tale she heard anon;
And soon by other tokens found,
   He was indeed her son.

But who's this hairy youth? she said;
   He much resembles thee:
The bear devour'd my younger son,
   Or sure that son were he.

Valentine and Ursine.

Madam, this youth with bears was bred,
  And rear'd within their den.
But recollect ye any mark
  To know your son again?

Upon his little side, quoth she,
  Was stamped a bloody rose.
Here, lady, see the crimson mark
  Upon his body grows!

Then clasping both her new-found sons
  She bath'd their cheeks with tears :
And soon towards her brother's court
  Her joyful course she steers.

What pen can paint king Pepin's joy,
  His sister thus restor'd!
And soon a messenger was sent
  To cheer her drooping lord :

Who came in haste with all his peers,
  To fetch her home to Greece ;
Where many happy years they reign'd
  In perfect love and peace.

Valentine and Ursine.

To them sir Ursine did succeed,
And long the sceptre bear.
Sir Valentine he stay'd in France,
And was his uncle's heir.

THE KING AND MILLER OF MANSFIELD.

PART THE FIRST.

ENRY, our royal king, would ride a hunting
  To the green forest so pleasant and fair;
  To see the harts skipping, and dainty does
   tripping:
Unto merry Sherwood his nobles repair:
Hawk and hound were unbound, all things prepar'd
For the game, in the same, with good regard.

All a long summer's day rode the king pleasantly,
 With all his princes and nobles each one;
Chasing the hart and hind, and the buck gallantly,
 Till the dark evening forc'd all to turn home.

Then at last, riding fast, he had lost quite
All his lords in the wood, late in the night.
Wandering thus wearily, all alone, up and down,
　　With a rude miller he met at the last:
Asking the ready way unto fair Nottingham ;
　　Sir, quoth the miller, I mean not to jest,
Yet I think, what I think, sooth for to say,
You do not lightly ride out of your way.

Why, what dost thou think of me, quoth our king merrily,
　　Passing thy judgment upon me so brief?
Good faith, said the miller, I mean not to flatter thee ;
　　I guess thee to be but some gentleman thief ;
Stand thee back, in the dark ; light not adown,
Lest that I presently crack thy knave's crown.

Thou dost abuse me much, quoth the king, saying thus ;
　　I am a gentleman ; lodging I lack.
Thou hast not, quoth th' miller, one groat in thy purse ;
　　All thy inheritance hangs on thy back.
I have gold to discharge all that I call ;*
If it be forty pence, I will pay all.

　　　　　* The king says this.

Miller of Mansfield.

If thou beest a true man, then quoth the miller,
  I swear by my toll-dish, I'll lodge thee all night.
Here's my hand, quoth the king; that was I ever.
  Nay, soft, quoth the miller, thou may'st be a sprite.
Better I'll know thee, ere hands we will shake;
With none but honest men hands will I take.

Thus they went all along unto the miller's house:
  Where they were seething of puddings and souse:
The miller first enter'd in; after him went the king;
  Never came he in so smoky a house.
Now, quoth he, let me see here what you are.
Quoth our king, look your fill, and do not spare.

I like well thy countenance; thou hast an honest face,
  With my son Richard this night thou shalt lie.
Quoth his wife, by my troth, it is a handsome youth;
  Yet it's best, husband, to deal warily.
Art thou no runaway, prythee, youth, tell?
Show me thy passport, and all shall be well.

Then our king presently, making low courtesy,
  With his hat in his hand, thus he did say;

I have no passport, nor never was servitor,
　But a poor courtier, rode out of my way :
And for your kindness here offered to me,
I will requite you in every degree.

Then to the miller his wife whispered secretly,
　Saying, It seemeth this youth's of good kin,
Both by his apparel, and eke by his manners ;
　To turn him out, certainly, were a great sin.
Yea, quoth he, you may see he hath some grace
When he doth speak to his betters in place.

Well, quo' the miller's wife, young man, ye're welcome here ;
　And, though I say it, well lodgèd shall be :
Fresh straw will I have laid on thy bed so brave,
　And good brown hempen sheets likewise, quoth she.
Aye, quoth the good man ; and when that is done,
Thou shalt lie with no worse than our own son.

This caus'd the king, suddenly, to laugh most heartily,
　Till the tears trickled fast down from his eyes.
Then to their supper were they set orderly,

THE KING AND THE MILLER OF MANSFIELD

With hot bag-puddings and good apple-pies;
Nappy ale, good and stale, in a brown bowl,
Which did about the board merrily trowl.

Here, quoth the miller, good fellow, I drink to thee,
  And to all courtiers, wherever they be.
I pledge thee, quoth our king, and thank thee heartily
  For my welcome in every good degree:
And here, in like manner, I drink to thy son.
Do then, quoth Richard, and quick let it come.

Wife, quoth the miller, fetch me forth lightfoot,
  And of his sweetness a little we'll taste.
A fair ven'son pasty brought she out presently.
  Eat, quoth the miller, but, sir, make no waste.
Here's dainty lightfoot! In faith, said the king,
I never before eat so dainty a thing.

I wis, quoth Richard, no dainty at all it is,
  For we do eat of it every day.
In what place, said our king, may be bought like to this?
  We never pay penny for it, by my fay:

From merry Sherwood we fetch it home here;
Now and then we make bold with our king's deer.

Then I think, said our king, that it is venison.
    Each fool, quoth Richard, full well may know that:
Never are we without two or three in the roof,
    Very well fleshed, and excellent fat:
But, prythee, say nothing wherever thou go;
We would not, for two pence, the king should it know.

Doubt not, then said the king, my promised secrecy;
    The king shall never know more on't for me.
A cup of lambs-wool * they drank unto him then,
    And to their beds they passed presently.
The nobles, next morning, went all up and down,
For to seek out the king in every town.

At last, at the miller's cot, soon they espy'd him out,
    As he was mounting upon his fair steed;
To whom they came presently, falling down on their knee;
    Which made the miller's heart wofully bleed;
Shaking and quaking, before him he stood,
Thinking he should have been hang'd, by the Rood.

    * Ale and roasted apples.

The king perceiving him fearfully trembling
  Drew forth his sword, but nothing he said :
The miller down did fall, crying before them all,
  Doubting the king would cut off his head.
But he, his kind courtesy for to requite,
Gave him great living, and dubb'd him a knight.

THE KING AND MILLER OF MANSFIELD.

PART THE SECOND.

WHEN as our royal king came home from Nottingham,
 And with his nobles at Westminster lay;
 Recounting the sports and pastimes they had taken,
 In this late progress along on the way;
Of them all, great and small, he did protest,
The miller of Mansfield's sport liked him best.

And now, my lords, quoth the king, I am determined
 Against St. George's next sumptuous feast,
That this old miller, our new confirmed knight,
 With his son Richard, shall here be my guest:
For, in this merriment, 'tis my desire
To talk with the jolly knight, and the young squire.

When as the noble lords saw the king's pleasantness,
  They were right joyful and glad in their hearts :
A pursuivant there was sent straight on the business,
  The which had oftentimes been in those parts.
When he came to the place, where they did dwell,
His message orderly then 'gan he tell.

God save your worship, then said the messenger,
  And grant your lady her own heart's desire ;
And to your son Richard good fortune and happiness ;
  That sweet, gentle, and gallant young squire.
Our king greets you well, and thus he doth say,
You must come to the court on St. George's day ;

Therefore, in any case, fail not to be in place.
  I wis, quoth the miller, this is an odd jest :
What should we do there ? faith, I am half afraid.
  I doubt, quoth Richard, to be hang'd at the least.
Nay, quoth the messenger, you do mistake ;
Our king he provides a great feast for your sake.

Then said the miller, By my troth, messenger,
  Thou hast contented my worship full well.

Hold, here are three farthings, to quite thy gentleness,
  For these happy tidings which thou dost tell.
Let me see, hear thou me; tell to our king,
We'll wait on his mastership in everything.

The pursuivant smiled at their simplicity,
  And, making many legs, took the reward ;
And his leave taking with great humility
  To the king's court again he repaired ;
Showing unto his grace, merry and free,
The knight's most liberal gift and bounty.

When he was gone away, thus 'gan the miller say,
  Here come expenses and charges indeed ;
Now must we needs be brave, tho' we spend all we have ;
  For of new garments we have great need :
Of horses and serving-men we must have store,
With bridles and saddles, and twenty things more.

Tush, sir John, quo' his wife, why should you fret, or frown ?
  You shall ne'er be at no charges for me ;
For I will turn and trim up my old russet gown,
  With everything else as fine as may be ;

And on our mill-horses swift we will ride,
With pillows and pannels, as we shall provide.

In this most stately sort, rode they unto the court,
  Their jolly son Richard rode foremost of all ;
Who set up, for good hap,* a cock's feather in his cap,
  And so they jetted † down to the king's hall ;
The merry old miller with hands on his side ;
His wife, like maid Marian, did mince at that tide.

The king and his nobles that heard of their coming,
  Meeting this gallant knight with his brave train ;
Welcome, sir knight, quoth he, with your gay lady :
  Good sir John Cockle, once welcome again :
And so is the squire of courage so free.
Quoth Dick, A bots on you ! do you know me ?

The king and his courtiers laugh at this heartily,
  While the king taketh them both by the hand ;
With the court-dames and maids, like to the queen of spades,
  The miller's wife did so orderly stand.

* For good luck.   † Strutted.

A milk-maid's courtesy at every word;
And down all the folks were set to the board.

There the king royally, in princely majesty,
    Sate at his dinner with joy and delight;
When they had eaten well, then he to jesting fell,
    And in a bowl of wine drank to the knight:
Here's to you both, in wine, ale, and beer;
Thanking you heartily for my good cheer.

Quoth sir John Cockle, I'll pledge you a pottle,
    Were it the best ale in Nottinghamshire:
But then said our king, now I think of a thing;
    Some of your lightfoot I would we had here.
Ho! ho! quoth Richard, full well I may say it,
'Tis knavery to eat it, and then to betray it.

Why art thou angry? quoth our king merrily;
    In faith I take it now very unkind:
I thought thou wouldst pledge me in ale and wine heartily.
    Quoth Dick, You are like to stay till I have din'd:
You feed us with twatling dishes so small;
Zounds, a black-pudding is better than all.

Thus in great merriment was the time wholly spent;
  And then the ladies preparèd to dance.
Old Sir John Cockle, and Richard, incontinent
  Unto their places the king did advance.
Here with the ladies such sport they did make,
The nobles with laughing did make their sides ache.

Many thanks for their pains did the king give them,
  Asking young Richard then, if he would wed;
Among these ladies free, tell me which liketh thee?
  Quoth he, Jugg Grumball, Sir, with the red head:
She's my love, she's my life, her will I wed;
She hath sworn I shall have her wedding bed.

Then sir John Cockle the king called unto him,
  And of merry Sherwood made him o'erseer;
And gave him out of hand three hundred pound yearly:
  Take heed now you steal no more of my deer:
And once a quarter let's here have your view;
And now, sir John Cockle, I bid you adieu.

R. CLAY, PRINTER, BREAD STREET HILL.